LANDMARK VISITORS GUIDE

Florida:
Gulf Coast

Don Philpott

LANDMARK VISITORS GUIDE

Florida:
Gulf Coast

Don Philpott

CONTENTS

FactFile

WELCOME TO FLORIDA: THE GULF COAST

Florida's 770-miles long (1,240km) Gulf Coast is one of the world's top tourist destinations, with award-winning beaches, bustling resorts, picturesque quays, countless attractions, great hotels and restaurants, out-of-the-way parks and nature reserves, fascinating wildlife and welcoming people. With near year-round sunshine, warm seas and mile upon mile of sandy beaches, what more could you want?

Getting There

By car:
The only way into Florida by land is from the north through either Georgia or Alabama. Interstate 95 runs all the way down the eastern coast, while Interstate 10, which starts in Los Angeles, enters Florida just west of Pensacola on the Gulf Coast. There are 'Welcome Centers' on all the

Above: Naples

main roads entering the state. Interstate 75 runs south along the length of the Gulf Coast, although it remains a few miles inland, while Highways 98, 19 and 41 hug the coastline for most of the journey down to southern Florida. The roads are excellent and fast, and if you want to slow down and explore the countryside there are many smaller side roads.

By bus:

Greyhound Lines operates services into the state and along the length of the Gulf Coast. The Greyhound Ameri-pass is a cheap and interesting means of travel, especially between cities, and is a great way to meet people. The scheme incorporates Greyhound and a number of other private bus and coach companies, and is fine for medium- and long-distance travel. Problems can occur, however, when you get off the Greyhound bus and then have to find public transport to take you to your final destination.

By train:

Amtrak runs rail services into the state and between many of the main cities. An Amtrak USA Railpass offers unlimited travel and as many stop-overs as you like for forty-five days, although some routes carry restrictions and you have to pay extra for sleeping-car accommodation. For further details ask your travel agent or write to Amtrak, 60 Massachusetts Avenue NE, Washington DC 20002 (℡ 202/906-3000 from outside North America, or 1-800-USA-RAIL from within the USA or Canada).

By air:

The main international arrival airport for the Gulf Coast is Tampa, which receives flights from all major overseas destinations. If you are staying along the southern Gulf Coast it may, however, be more convenient to fly into Miami and then drive the remaining distance. Fort Myers also receives some international flights and there are local airports at Sarasota, Clearwater, Tallahassee, Panama Beach and Pensacola. Competition on Florida routes is intense and pricing is very competitive, so it pays to shop around. Air fares are highest at peak times (Christmas, Easter and the summer holidays), while bargains can often be found at other times of the year, even if it means a brief stop-over in another US city

rather than a direct flight. Package deals generally afford the best value. If you want the freedom to roam or to pick your own accommodation, opt for fly-drive. Always ask your travel agent what special offers, hotel discounts and other incentives are available. If you fly on a regular basis, join the free 'frequent flyer' schemes operated by most major airlines.

By sea:

Cruise ships sail to Florida regularly. The Intracoastal Waterway runs through Card and Barnes Sounds to Florida Bay, and is suitable for vessels with a draft of 5ft (1.5m) or less. Hawk Channel is the oceanside route, with a line of buoys marking the safe passage through the reefs and Keys.

When To Go

Any time of the year is a good time to visit the Gulf Coast, although during the winter months the weather is considerably warmer in the south than in the north. The coastal resorts are very busy from Christmas to May but are fast becoming a year-round destination, with many visitors spending time at the attractions in central Florida before heading for the beaches of the Gulf Coast.

Climate

The year-round good weather is the main reason people flock to Florida's Gulf Coast in their millions. There are two seasons: hot, humid and wet summers from April to September; and warm and mostly dry weather for the rest of the year. The average annual temperature throughout the state tops 80°F (27°C), with January being the coolest month and July and August the hottest. Even during the hottest weather there are usually welcome inshore breezes from the Gulf, which help to keep you cool. Evening temperatures drop only a few degrees, making the region ideal for moonlight strolls. Having said that, the hottest temperature ever recorded in Florida was 109°F (42°C) in 1931 near Monticello, to the east of Tallahassee, while the lowest was -2°F (-17°C), recorded in Tallahassee in 1899.

Sustained cold spells are rare, especially in the south, although evening and night-time temperatures can dip during the winter. Occasional frosts occur in the north during the winter but are almost unheard of in the south, and even when there is a frost, it is usual for the rising sun to quickly lift the temperature.

Average annual rainfall is 40–45in (102–114cm) per year. In the late afternoon or early evening during the summer months there are often spectacular electrical storms and torrential downpours, usually accompanied by thunder. These deluges rarely last long and can often be over in a few minutes. They can also be so localized that an area which has remained dry all day may stand just a few hundred yards from the scene of a torrential downpour.

When it does rain it generally pours, which is why most homes in Florida do not have gutters: they simply would not be able to cope with the volume of water. If you are caught out in one of these downpours, especially if there is lightning, seek shelter at once. You normally get some warning before it starts raining as the wind usually picks up and the temperature drops. As soon as the rain stops, however, both the temperature and humidity pick up again, and the rainwater soon evaporates.

If you are driving when it starts to rain heavily, turn on your headlights and windshield wipers and reduce your speed. Exercise the greatest caution because the roads often flood, blinding spray is thrown up and the danger of aquaplaning increases, especially if you have to brake quickly.

There is a risk of hurricanes any time between June and November, with September the highest-risk month. However, the risk of a hurricane actually coming ashore is not great. The most severe storm to hit Florida for decades

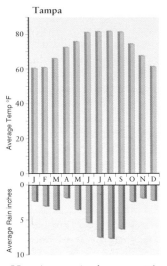

Tampa

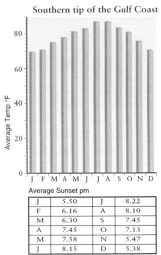

Southern tip of the Gulf Coast

Average Sunset pm

J	5.50	J	8.22
F	6.16	A	8.10
M	6.30	S	7.45
A	7.45	O	7.13
M	7.58	N	5.47
J	8.15	D	5.38

was Hurricane Andrew, with winds of 164mph (264kph), which devastated Homestead, an area south of Miami in August 1992. Apart from fierce high winds and towering seas, torrential and sustained rainfall is the major feature associated with tropical storms and hurricanes. Florida's wettest day was in September 1950 during hurricane activity, when 38.5in (98cm) of rain fell during a twenty-four-hour period close to Cedar Key on the Gulf Coast.

On average, a hurricane hits Florida about once every five years, although the vast majority of these cause only minimal damage. The state can also expect to be affected by an offshore hurricane about once every two years. Because of the potential threat of hurricanes, Florida has a very so-phisticated tracking and alert system. All tropical storms are monitored and their positions announced on local radio and television stations. In the unlikely event of a hurricane posing a serious threat during your holiday, listen to the media for the latest instructions.

Geography

Florida covers an area of almost 58,665sq miles (152,066sq km), most of this forming a peninsula that juts out from the south-east corner of the continent to separate the Atlantic Ocean from the Gulf of Mexico. It is the fourth largest state in the US and the most southerly of the mainland states. Its most northerly point is still 100 miles (161km) south of

Above: *The Kumba Coaster at Busch Gardens, Tampa* **Below:** *Lee Island Coast has wonderful beaches for families with children*

the most southerly point in California, and more than 1,000 miles (1,610km) south of the French Riviera. It borders only two states – Georgia and Alabama to the north – and its capital, Tallahassee, is located in the north-western area known as the Panhandle.

The highest point in the state is found in the far north just south of the border with Alabama, and at 345ft (105m) above sea-level it is, in Florida terms, a veritable mountain. Most of the land lies less than 100ft (30m) above sea-level. Underneath the topsoil lies a bed of limestone, and erosion of this has carved out the thousands of lakes, caves and springs for which the state is so famous. There are more than 30,000 lakes, 105 state parks, 7 national parks, 3 national forests, around 1,000 golf courses, 17 greyhound tracks and 6 horse-racing venues. In addition, Florida is home to some of the world's top tourist attractions, including Walt Disney World, Sea World and Busch Gardens, all of which lie within an hour or so of the Gulf Coast. When you also take into account its fabulous beaches, it is no wonder that Florida is the world's number-one tourist destination.

Flora and Fauna

More than half of Florida is covered by forests, and more than 300 types of trees have been identified together with over 3,500 other plants. The hardwood forests of the north give way to the tropical forests and mangrove swamps of the south, with oak, pine, cypress, palm and mangrove predominating. You will also find Caribbean imports in the south such as mahogany, gumbo-limbo, palms and palmettos. For most of the year in the south there is a blaze of tropical blooms including royal poinciana, poinsettia, gardenia, jasmine, bougainvillaea, trumpet vine, oleander, hibiscus, orchids, flamboyant, morning glory and azalea. There are also trees bearing a wide range of edible fruits and nuts from mango, papaya, carambola, banana and Key lime to coconut. Florida's state tree is the sabal palm, while its state flower is the orange blossom.

Note that the manchineel tree, which can be found on many beaches, has a number of effective defensive mechanisms which can prove very painful. The trees vary from just a few feet to more than 30ft (9m) in height, and have wide-spreading, deep-forked boughs with small, dark green leaves and yellow stems, and fruit that resembles small, green apples. If you examine the leaves carefully without touching them, you will notice a small pinhead-sized raised dot at the junction of the leaf and leaf stalk. The apple-like fruit is very poisonous, and sap from the tree causes very painful blisters. Indeed, it is so toxic that early Caribs are said to have dipped their arrowheads in it. Sap is released if a leaf or branch is broken, especially after rain. Avoid contact with the tree, don't sit under one or on a fallen branch, and do not eat the fruit. If you do get sap on your skin, run into the sea and wash it off as quickly as possible.

Florida also has a rich and diverse wildlife, including about a hundred species of mammals and many of the rarer animals – such as the panther, black bear and Florida crocodile – are protected. You are quite likely to see armadillos, skunks and porcupines shuffling along roadsides late at night, and squirrels, raccoons and opossums are all common. Otter and mink live close to inland waterways, white-tailed deer live in the woodlands, there are a dozen species of bat, and wild boar roam the swamps and woods the length of the state. There are also sixty species of snake (the four poisonous types are the rattlesnake, coral, cottonmouth moccasin and copperhead) and many other reptiles, of which the alligator is the most celebrated.

Florida has about 420 species of birds, the state bird being the mockingbird. Graceful white cattle egrets can be spotted everywhere, and most holidaymakers take home with them memories of turkey vultures soaring effortlessly overhead, or of the aerial acrobatics of pelicans before they plunge into the Gulf after fish. There are hundreds of species of insects, from irritating mosquitoes and tiny black flies (no-see-'ems), to spiders and, very rarely, scorpions. Some of the insects can be a nuisance, but a little care is all that is needed to avoid trouble. If you are in self-catering accommodation, clean any sticky spills or sugar ants will soon invade. Ants abound in Florida, and it is prudent to make sure the ground is ant-free before sitting down as some species give a nasty sting. One example is the fire ant, so called because of the intense burning sensation experienced after you have been stung. Other insects to be wary of are hornets and wasps (both aggressive), mosquitoes, scorpions and some spiders – in particular, the black widow, tarantula and the brown recluse or fiddleback, all of which bite or sting.

The warm waterways sometimes play host to the gentle and delightful manatee, which needs all the protection it can get, while bottlenose dolphins are plentiful and can be seen in coastal waters. Less delightful are the many species of jellyfish that thrive in the warm sea. The Portugese man-of-war is the most dangerous jellyfish and treatment should be sought quickly by anyone who is stung.

A Naturalist's Guide

In the north-west of the state, rolling hills run across the Panhandle to the Gulf of Mexico. The long-leaf pine forests here are home to black bears, white-tailed deer, fox squirrels, some coyote (which have migrated down from the north), gophers and tortoises. They are also home to the largest population of endangered red-cockaded woodpecker in the US. The Panhandle is criss-crossed by some eighteen rivers and hundreds of creeks, where you can see turtles, river otters and beavers. The surrounding marshes, hardwoods and cypress woods teem with bobcats, grey foxes and grey squirrels, while bats and blind salamanders inhabit the numerous limestone caves. The sandy barrier islands off the Panhandle coast offer refuge for spring migrating birds and butterflies, as well as many species of nesting birds. To the east, the Suwannee River basin boasts one of the greatest concentrations of clear-water springs in the world, while to the south lies the Big Bend Coast, whose huge areas of marsh and seagrass meadows are home to tens of thousands of wintering waterfowl. Inland there are dense pine forests and swamps, also rich in wildlife.

The central Gulf Coast area has a variety of habitats, from pine sandhills to vast, dense woodlands. There are many spring-fed rivers and streams here, especially in the north, the largest of which are home to significant numbers of manatees during the winter months. Scattered among the pine woodlands are 'hammocks' – areas of higher land covered in dense vegetation – where you can see white-tailed deer, grey squirrels, red-shouldered hawks, barred owls and many species of songbird. To the north along the Gulf Coast are salt marshes, while mangrove forests and a chain of barrier islands lie to the south. This region has many state and county parks, all with excellent facilities for watching wildlife at close quarters. DeSoto County has large areas of dry prairie, sand dunes and scrub flatlands where you can spot crested caracaras, sandhill cranes, burrowing owls and colonies of waders, including a number of rare species.

The south-western region runs from just north of Punta Gorda to Ten Thousand Islands. In the north, pine flats flood during the rainy season to produce numerous small ponds. The landscape is slightly more undulating to the south, with pine flats, oak- and cabbage-palm ham-

Above: *Florida alligators can grow up to 15ft (4.6m) long*

mocks, sand-pine scrub, cypress domes and dry prairies. There are enormous wetland and forest preserves here, as well as the western Everglades, the last major habitat of the rare Florida panther. The region's barrier islands, mangrove bays and estuaries are rich in marine life, and are also home to many species of nesting wading birds, ospreys and bald eagles. In addition, manatees can be seen here, especially to the south around Ten Thousand Islands, where you can also see dolphins, rays and sharks. This area – the western edge of the Everglades National Park – is accessible only by boat or canoe.

The final area, the far south, is dominated by the Everglades, these extending over 1 million acres (400,000 hectares) to the Gulf Coast, and taking in Flamingo and Everglades City. Sea turtles still nest on a few protected beaches, while west of Lake Okeechobee, Florida's largest lake, you can see large numbers of the spectacular black and white swallow-tailed kites which gather here in midsummer before migrating south. Aside from the scores of species of wading birds (including storks, herons, egrets, spoonbills and ibis) seen in the Everglades, this is also one of the best places to see really large American alligators. The Everglades remain unparalleled, and despite having suffered damage through farming and over-exploitation they are still magnificent and continue to teem with wildlife.

There are rich pickings along Florida's beaches if you are a seashell collector. Pink conch shells up to 8in (20cm) long are sometimes washed up, while the rare Triton's trumpet can measure up to 9in (22cm). Common shells include frog-shells, distorsios, volutes, tulips, murex, cones, olives, marginellas, cowries, augers and the Florida horse conch, the state's official shell, which can grow up to 24in (61cm) long. Crown conch shells can be found near mangrove swamps and sheltered bays, while the smallest variety of crown conch, *Melongena corona*, can sometimes be found on the islands in the Gulf.

The People

The population of Florida lies at just under 13 million, although this swells every year as around 42 million holidaymakers descend on the 'Sunshine State', the world's top tourist destination. The main population centres on the Gulf Coast are Pensacola and Panama City in the north, with Tallahassee, the capital, lying about 20 miles (32km) inland. Tampa, Clearwater and St Petersburg form the main metropolitan conurbation on the central Gulf Coast, while Sarasota and Fort Myers are the main cities to the south. The whole of the

coastline is developing rapidly, with many of the new towns and communities on or close to the Gulf expanding fast.

Food and Drink

There is a wide range of wonderful fresh foods to enjoy in Florida, from giant Gulf shrimps to Key lime pie. There are exotic fruits such as mango, papaya and carambola, and the freshest of fresh fish and shellfish. There are fast-food outlets for those looking for meals on the run, although one of the treats of Florida's Gulf Coast is being able to dine leisurely out of doors, enjoying both the sea views and the seafood. Most restaurants offer wonderful salad bars and all-inclusive specials which make eating out more affordable, while the all-you-can-eat breakfasts, lunches and dinners are ideal for parents who have to feed the huge appetites of growing children!

Seafood is eaten grilled, boiled, baked and sautéed. It is used to make delicious soups, chowders and stews, while lobster and crab are often served cold with a mayonnaise sauce – delicious! You will come across yellowtail and mutton snappers, groupers, tiny grunts, dolphins (this is actually the fish known as mahi mahi, not the mammal), spiny lobsters, oysters, conch, giant pink shrimps and delicious stone crabs, all caught in local waters. The latter are 'harvested' by local fishermen, who often remove only one of the crab's large claws. The crabs are then returned to the sea where they grow another claw within a few months. Conch (pronounced 'konk') are highly nutritious, and can be served grilled, minced to form conch burgers, fried in batter as fritters, or eaten raw in salads.

Another culinary treat is to sample the numerous different ethnic cuisines available – from Cuban to Chinese, from Caribbean to Italian, and from German to Japanese. In Ybor City and elsewhere you can try Cuban-inspired *lechon*: roast pork flavoured with garlic and tart oranges to produce a unique flavour. Other dishes include *ropa vieja* (literally 'old clothes'), which is a beef dish, and *picadillo*, a hamburger-caper-raisin mixture served with a savoury sauce. All dishes are usually served with boiled white or yellow rice, the latter flavoured with either saffron or *bihol*, and black beans. Bahamian fish stew with grits is served in the south near the Keys, and many southern state specialities have been adapted by Floridians. Hush puppies, for instance, are made from mashed, shelled black-eyed peas rather than ground cornmeal, and are called *bollos* (pronouned 'boy-ohs').

Local puddings include 'flans' such as baked and caramelized custard, guava shells stuffed with cream cheese, and fresh tropical fruits perhaps served with tropical-fruit-flavoured ice-cream. And then there is Key lime pie, Florida's official dessert, made with condensed or evaporated milk and the juice and grated rind of the piquant Key limes.

History

Early Years

Many Indian tribes were already occupying different parts of Florida when the first European explorers arrived: the Apalachees, Tocobagas and Timucuans in the west; the fierce, nomadic Calusa, allegedly 7ft (2m) tall, who were masters of the Everglades; and a number of smaller tribes, most of whom stayed on the move to avoid the others. Imported diseases, slavery and war soon took their toll, however, so that by 1750 almost all the Indians had been wiped out.

Florida was named by Juan Ponce de León, who landed on the Atlantic Coast somewhere near present-day St Augustine on Easter Monday, 1513. He thought he had discovered a new island in the Bahamas and claimed it for Spain, naming it Florida after *Pascua Florida*, the traditional Spanish Feast of Flowers

Following Page: St Pete's Beach

held during Easter. De León returned with another expedition in 1521 with the intention of establishing a settlement, but Indian attacks forced him to withdraw.

The first permanent Spanish settlement, and the oldest European settlement anywhere in the USA, was established by Pedro Menéndez de Avilés at St Augustine in 1565. A year earlier, and about 50 miles (80km) away, a group of Protestant Huguenots under René Goulaine de Laudonniér had built Fort Caroline at the mouth of the St Johns River, but it was overrun by Menéndez in 1565 and renamed San Mateo. The Spanish colonization then spread through northern Florida via a chain of forts, and they dominated the region for the next 150 years. The English at this time were colonizing much further north, and one of their few incursions into the region was a raid by Sir Francis Drake on St Augustine in 1586.

English Interlude

By the early eighteenth century English colonists from Georgia and South Carolina started to move south, attacking the Spanish settlements in their path. At the same time the French were attacking Spanish settlements in the west, and in 1719 they captured Pensacola. In 1763, after the Seven Years War, a deal was struck between England and Spain ceding Florida to the English in return for Cuba. Florida was divided into two territories, each with its own capital: East Florida, administered from St Augustine; and West Florida, with its headquarters in Pensacola. However, plans to colonize the territories were disrupted by the American War of Independence. Although both territories remained loyal to the English crown, their remoteness and the confusion caused by the war allowed the Spanish to return and reclaim Florida for themselves.

Indian Wars

A period of intense colonization then started, but the new settlers were in almost constant conflict with the Indians, who had also moved in from the north to populate the region. This was the time of the Indian Wars. Creek Indians and other tribes became known as Seminoles, from the Spanish word for 'wanderers'. The First Seminole War started in 1817 and ended four years later when Spain sold the territory to the USA. East and West Florida were then united and Tallahassee declared the new capital.

The Seminoles who had survived the war were ordered to leave Florida for the Indian Territory. Their chief, Osceola, refused, thereby precipitating President Andrew Jackson to launch the Second Seminole War in 1835. The bloody seven-year war left most of the Indians dead, with a few hundred escaping into the Everglades and the rest being herded on to the Indian Territory hundreds of miles away to the north-west.

Today, there are 2,000 Native Americans living in and around the Everglades. About three-quarters of them are descendants of the Seminoles, the rest being Miccosukees. It was only in 1962 that official relations between the Native Americans and the US government were resumed.

Statehood and Development

Three years after the end of the Second Seminole War, Florida became the twenty-seventh state of the USA. The population of around 55,000 was concentrated in the north and the economy relied almost entirely on agricultural plantations. Then, in the 1880s, tourism came to Florida. A railroad was driven down the east coast followed by another down the west, and resorts and industry developed.

Marshland and swamps were drained for farming, roads were built and new communities sprang up. Many ethnic groups settled in the state, including Spaniards and Cubans around Tampa, Greek immigrants in Tarpon Springs, Jewish émigrés in Miami and Slovaks in Masaryktown. The property boom lasted until the Depression,

and was then rejuvenated when the United States entered World War II and chose Florida as its good-weather training ground. The property market took off once again and things have never looked back since.

Tourism plays the most important role in the state's economy today, but agriculture, mining and industry are all key players. In 1968 the state government, conscious of the rapid population growth, introduced a new constitution that accommodated both the needs of an expanding population and the necessity to preserve the state's rich natural habitat. Today, the population of Florida is still increasing faster than that of any other state, and the property boom continues at a frantic pace.

KEY TO RESTAURANT RATINGS

$$$	Up-market
$$	Good
$	Budget

PENSACOLA TO CLEARWATER AND ST PETERSBURG

1

The sights and towns in this section follow Florida's Gulf Coast east along the Panhandle and south down the peninsula as far as Clearwater and St Petersburg.

Perdido Key and the Gulf Islands National Seashore

As you cross over the border from Alabama into north-western Florida you come across one of the state's best-kept secrets: the fabulous beaches and rolling dunes that run from Perdido Key to Pensacola Beach, Fort Walton

Beach and then simply carry on for mile after mile. Remember that this western end of the Panhandle is in the Central Time Zone, one hour behind most of Florida and six hours behind GMT.

Perdido Key is the westernmost island in Florida, and is linked to both Alabama and Florida by high-rise bridges. The island is

Above: Panama City Beach has miles of pure white sand

noted for its wonderful beaches – consistently voted among the best in the country – and has a good range of accommodation and restaurants as well as some fun old-time night spots. It is a year-round destination and is popular with the 'snow birds' who head down from the north to spend their winters in the sun. Perdido Key also hosts an annual ten-day festival of song-writers every November, when the nation's top song-writers perform their works and hold seminars.

Perdido Key (meaning 'Lost Island') was first discovered by the Spanish in 1693, and although the discerning have sought out its beaches for more than a century, it is only in the last decade or so that it has become popular. While there has been a lot of recent development, almost three-quarters of the key is protected by either federal or state parks, which means that there is plenty of access to secluded areas for those who want to roam or find a quiet place of their own to sunbathe.

The parks also provide covered picnic areas, toilets and other amenities.

The nearby Big Lagoon State Recreation Area, with its marshes and woodlands, also offers a wide range of activities and attractions, including campsites, hiking trails and nature walks, an observation tower, picnic areas and pop concerts.

In the nationwide beach ratings, Perdido Key was rated twelfth. These internationally accepted listings are compiled by Maryland geologist Dr Stephen Leatherman ('Dr Beach'), and rate beaches by the softness and cleanliness of the sand, water quality, number of sunny days, smell, pests, access, crowds and crime, as well as more than forty other factors. In addition to the beaches facing the Gulf, Perdido Key offers the more tranquil River Perdido on its opposite shore. The contrast makes the island ideal for all sorts of family watersports, including fishing, water-skiing, snorkelling, surfing and swimming.

Santa Rosa Island is the home of **Pensacola Beach**, and offers mile after mile of unspoiled white-sand beaches, warm, clear, blue-green waters, a wide variety of restaurants and nightlife, and a strong flavour of history. Santa Rosa is a barrier island that was once totally protected as a federal reserve, and commercial development is still banned from much of it today. The beaches stretch for 16 miles (26km), and include several that are popular with sunseekers. The waters off shore teem with motorboats and yachts, there is great fishing from boat or shore, and there is parasailing if you want a bird's-eye view of the beaches.

The **Gulf Islands National Seashore**, founded in 1971, covers almost 29,000 acres (12,000 hectares) of pristine beaches, dunes, coastal marshes and scrub uplands. It runs for 150 miles (242km), a third of which lie in north-western Florida, and includes the barrier islands to the south of Pensacola, which can be reached by Highway 98.

Across the causeway is Gulf Breeze and, to the east, **Naval Live Oaks**. This area was set aside by President John Quincy Adams to ensure the availability of live oaks which were used to build some of the most famous wooden ships in American history. The resulting undisturbed environment has since become home to very large numbers of birds and animals.

The road then continues over Santa Rosa Sound to Pensacola Beach and Highway 399, which runs along Santa Rosa Island and through the Gulf Islands National Seashore. The ruins of **Fort Pickens**, which figured in the Civil War, and several concrete batteries lie at the western end of the island. The fort was one of three built between 1829 and 1834 to protect Pensacola Harbor during the Civil War, and it was here that the Apache leader Geronimo was imprisoned in 1886. It now houses a visitor centre, museum and auditorium. Open: daily; guided tours. Small admission charge. © 904/934-2635

From Fort Pickens itself you can spot bottlenose dolphins, brown pelicans and many species of sea- and shore birds. Mice, raccoons, rabbits and snakes live among the dunes, while skunks, opossums and raccoons are nocturnal visitors to the campsite which lies 2 miles (3km) east of the fort. Egrets, herons and bitterns are found in the marshes, where you may also spot signs of beavers.

Blocks of up-market condominiums and expensive houses overlook the Gulf just down the road from the fort, while the central business district east of Fort Pickens offers several blocks of restaurants, nightclubs, souvenir shops and an amusement park. The island hosts many special events, including the annual Snowfest, Mardi Gras, seafood festival and Bushwhacker Weekend. Bicycles, scooters, jet-skis and other transportation can be hired on the island, and there are bike paths as well as trails for joggers and roller-skaters.

Pensacola

Pensacola was first settled by Don Tristan de Luna, who landed in 1559 with 1,400 troops but stayed less than two years. The first permanent settlement did not take place until 1698, when Don Andres de Ariola arrived with 350 soldiers and built Fort San Carlos to protect the Spanish colonists from the Indians. Since then the town has flown the flags of Spain, France, England, the Confederate states and the United States – hence its name 'City of Five Flags' – and its government has changed hands thirteen times. In 1841, the British used the harbour as a base for their war with the United States, but they withdrew when the city was attacked by Andrew Jackson. It was also Jackson who finalized the agreement by which Spain sold Florida to the US in 1821; Plaza Ferdinand VII in Park Square is believed to have been the place where the deal was struck. Pensacola remained the territorial capital until 1822, with Andrew Jackson the first territorial governor of Florida.

The Seville Square Historic District is bounded to the north by Government Street and to the east by Alcaniz Street, and has many fine nineteenth-century buildings that have been restored and now house shops, restaurants, museums and art galleries. During the annual Fiesta of Five Flags, which takes place in early June, the square bustles with parades, art shows and a re-enactment of de Luna's landing. Palafont Place is another charming area where the historic buildings have been well restored.

The city boasts a large number of attractions, many of them associated with the huge US Naval Air Station. This is a training centre for electronic warfare, the home of the Blue Angels precision flying team, and the home port of the aircraft-carrier USS *Forrestal*. There are guided tours of the ship at weekends when it is in dock. In addition, the waterfront community offers a wide range of accommodation and a great choice of restaurants and sights, including more than 40 miles (65km) of shoreline. The Pensacola Tourist Information Centre, at the foot of the 3miles (5km) bay bridge, offers free information about a self-guided tour of the city; markers point out historic sites in the downtown, Seville and North Hill areas.

The best shopping areas include Cordova Mall on N Ninth Avenue, which has over 120 stores, and University Mall on N Davis Highway, which features more than a hundred stores.

The city and surrounding area host many annual festivals, including the downtown Greek Festival, the Beatlemania and Beach Festival, the Great Gulf Coast Arts Festival at Seville Square, the Pensacola Interstate Fair, the Blue Angels Homecoming Air Show, the Fiesta of the Five Flags and SpringFest, which brings nationally famous musicians to downtown Pensacola for a week-long street festival.

Pensacola Sights

The **Bluffs** (Scenic Highway near Summit Boulevard) offers fantastic views over Escambia Bay. There are a number of walkways offering various panoramas and photo opportunities.

Charles Lavalle House (203 E Church Street) dates from 1820 and as such is one of the city's oldest houses. It is built in typical Gulf Coast Creole cottage style.

The **Civil War Soldiers Museum** (108 S Palafox Street) houses Civil War exhibits and memorabilia, including life-size dioramas depicting battlefield scenes, contemporary medicine and the daily lives of soldiers. Open: Monday to Saturday 10am–4.30pm. Small admission charge. ✆ 904/469-1900.

Clara Barkley Dorr House (corner of S Adams Street and Church Street) is a fine example of Classical Revival architecture. The house was built in 1871 and contains period furnishings.

The **Edward Ball Nature Walk** (on the campus of the University

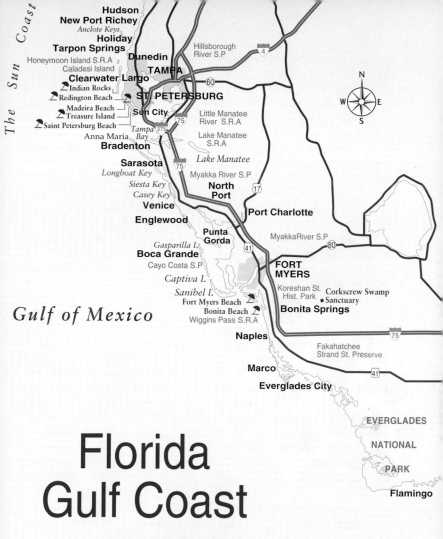

Hudson
New Port Richey
Anclote Keys
Holiday
Tarpon Springs
Honeymoon Island S.R.A
Caladesi Island
Dunedin
TAMPA
Hillsborough
River S.P
Clearwater Largo
Indian Rocks
Redington Beach
ST. PETERSBURG
60
Madeira Beach
Treasure Island
Saint Petersburg Beach
Sun City
Tampa
Little Manatee
River S.R.A
75
Anna Maria
Bay
275
Lake Manatee
S.R.A
Bradenton
Lake Manatee
Sarasota
Longboat Key
75
Myakka River S.P
North
Port
17
Siesta Key
Casey Key
Venice
Port Charlotte
Englewood
Punta
Gorda
MyakkaRiver S.P
80
Gasparilla I.
Boca Grande
41
Cayo Costa S.P
FORT
MYERS
Captiva I.
Koreshan St.
Hist. Park
Corkscrew Swamp
Sanctuary
Sanibel I.
Fort Myers Beach
Bonita Beach
Bonita Springs
Gulf of Mexico
Wiggins Pass S.R.A
75
Naples
Fakahatchee
Strand St. Preserve
Marco
41
Everglades City
EVERGLADES

NATIONAL

PARK
Flamingo

N
W E
S

Florida
Gulf Coast

0   20   40   60 miles

0   20 40 60 80Km

of West Florida) follows a bayou where you can feed fish and turtles.

Historic Pensacola Village is a fascinating collection of well-restored nineteenth-century buildings. Open: daily 10am–4pm from Easter to Labor Day (end of September), and Monday to Saturday 10am–4pm during the rest of the year. ✆ 904/444-8905

Julee Cottage (Zaragoza and Barracks streets) is the former home of Julee Panton, a free black woman, and was built in 1804.

The **Museum of Commerce** (next to the Museum of Industry; see below) has a fascinating reconstruction of a turn-of-the-century Pensacola street, with printers, grocers, a train depot, a fuel station and general stores.

The **Museum of Industry** (Zaragoza and Tarragona streets) is housed in a building which dates from 1877, and traces the history of the region through old maps, documents, furniture, fabrics and costumes, as well as household and maritime items.

The **National Museum of Naval Aviation** at the US Naval Air Station, is the third-largest air and space museum in the world, and is devoted to the history of naval aviation and space exploration. There are more than a hundred space- and aircraft on show, including the NC-4 Flying Boat which in 1919 became the first plane to cross the Atlantic, World War II fighters and the Skylab Command Module. There are also displays on space exploration, a replica of a World War II aircraft-carrier and hands-on exhibits. Open: daily 9am–5pm. ✆ 904/452-3604

The **Pensacola Historical Museum** (405 S Adams Street) is housed in the Old Christ Church and contains local history exhibits dating back to early Indian settlements. Built in 1832, the church served as a Federal barracks, prison, hospital and chapel during the Civil War. Open: Monday to Saturday 9am–4.30pm. Small admission charge. ✆ 904/433-1559.

The **Pensacola Museum of Art** is housed in the old city jail, and has local and travelling art exhibits. ✆ 904/432-6247

Pensacola US Naval Air Station (at the southern end of Navy Boulevard) is open daily between 9am and 5pm; visitor maps and passes are available at the main gate. Attractions include Fort Barrancas, a sixteenth-century fort with dry moat and drawbridge that was built by the Spanish. Open: daily 9.30am–5pm from April to October, and daily 10.30am–4pm during the rest of the year; there are guided tours.

Pensacola Zoo (east of the city near Gulf Breeze) is home to more than 800 animals, many of them endangered species from around the world, as well as a lovely botanical garden. Open: daily

9am–4pm (5pm in the summer).
© 904/932-2229

Plaza Ferdinand VII (Park Square) was part of the original Spanish settlement and has many fine old buildings. There is a statue here commemorating Andrew Jackson.

TT Wentforth Junior Florida State Museum (330 S Jefferson Street) is housed in the restored Italian Renaissance Pensacola Town Hall. It contains exhibits on the history and development of western Florida and also has a children's section. Open: Monday to Saturday 10am–4pm year round, and on Sunday 1pm–4pm between Easter and September. Admission includes entry to the Historic Pensacola Village).
© 904/444-8905

Veteran's Memorial Park (Bayfront Parkway near 9th Avenue) features The Wall South, the nation's first full-name replica of the Vietnam Veteran's Memorial in Washington DC. This sombre memorial lists the names of the 58,204 men and women who lost their lives in the war. Open: around the clock.

The **Wildlife Rescue and Sanctuary** (105 N South Street) offers nature-lovers the chance to see injured wild animals and birds being brought in for treatment. Open: Wednesday to Saturday 10am–2pm. Donations welcome.
© 904/433-9453

Pensacola Restaurants

The Angus
($$; Cajun), 1101 Scenic Highway, Pensacola.
© 904/432-0539

Aroma of Mandarin
($; Oriental),
4801 N 9th Street, Pensacola
© 904/476-8899

Boy on a Dolphin
($$; seafood and steaks),
400 Pensacola Beach Boulevard.
© 904/932-7954

Chris's Seafood Grill
($$; seafood), 47 Gulf Breeze Parkway, Gulf Breeze
© 850/438-7711

Cuco's Mexican Restaurante
($), 7100 N Davis Highway, Pensacola.
© 904/474-1611

Flounder's Chowder and Ale House
($$; seafood and steaks),
800 Quietwater Beach Road, Pensacola Beach
© 904/932-2003

Founaris Bros Greek Restaurant
($), 1015 N 9th Avenue, Pensacola
© 904/432-0629

Above: *The National Museum of Naval Aviation, Pensacola*
Below: *Shopping Mall, Panama City*

Gauthier's
($$$; seafood and international),
14110 Perdido Key Drive,
Perdido Key
✆ 904/492-1994

Hall's Seafood
($$), 920 E Gregory Street,
Pensacola
✆ 904/438-9019

Jamie's French Restaurant
($$$), 424 E Zarragossa Street
✆ 904/434-2911

Marchelo's Italian Restaurant
($$), 620 S Navy Boulevard,
Pensacola
✆ 904/456-5200

Oscar's Restaurant
($$; steak and international),
2805 West Cervantes Street,
Pensacola
✆ 904/432-8388

Mesquite Charlie's
($$; steak, seafood)
5901 North 'W' Street,
Pensacola.
✆ 904/434-0498

Skopelos on the Bay
($$; steak, seafood and Greek),
670 Scenic Highway,
Pensacola.
✆ 904/432-6565

Smokey's Real Pit BBQ
($; American), 6475 N
Pensacola Boulevard, Pensacola.
✆ 904/478-0860
Driving east from Pensacola

Beach along Santa Rosa Island takes you to **Navarre Beach**. Navarre town and the Welcome Center are located on the mainland opposite across the Santa Rosa Sound, which serves as the Intracoastal Waterway, although the two are also connected by the Navarre Bridge. Navarre Beach boasts 343 days of sunshine a year and surprisingly mild winters, with temperatures rarely dipping below 50°F (10°C). The beach is secluded and largely undeveloped, and is best known for its soft, sugar-fine white sand, the end result of Appalachian Mountain quartz crystals that have been broken down, washed, bleached and then polished into millions of grains of sand. The clear, turquoise waters lap against miles of bays, lagoons and beaches which offer swimming, boating, water-skiing, sailing and jet-skiing. The Santa Rosa Sound is internationally renowned for its windsurfing.

There is excellent fresh- and saltwater fishing for bonita, speckled trout, king mackerel, pompano and many other species; deep-sea charter boats are available for half- and full-day trips. The area also offers great diving, with its clear waters, colourful tropical marine life and underwater wrecks. There are three championship eighteen-hole golf courses within a ten-minute drive of Navarre Beach: the Club at Hidden Creek; and two courses at

Tiger Point, which overlooks Santa Rosa Sound.

Because most of Navarre Beach is part of the Gulf Islands National Seashore, it is protected and so remains largely in its natural state. A 0.5 mile (0.8km) boardwalk, called the Nature Walk, runs along the shores of Santa Rosa Sound and takes in a public park, boat dock, amphitheatre, marina, exhibition pavilion, picnic areas, shops and waterfront restaurants. The centrepiece is a spring-fed pond that hosts native waterfowl and aquatic species, and which is set in an area of natural wetlands. The development that does occur is strictly controlled and has to be sensitive to the environment. There is a range of accommodation, from resort hotels and motels to luxury condominiums, town houses, beach houses and waterfront campsites.

Navarre Restaurants

Cowboy's Steakhouse
($$; seafood and steaks),
8673 Navarre Parkway
℗ 904/939-0502

Fish House Restaurant
($), 8649 Gulf Boulevard
℗ 850/939-1440

Hazel's Country Kitchen
($; American),
8133 Verano Street
℗ 904/939-3437
Sailor's Grill

($), 1451 Navarre Beach Boulevard
℗ 904/939-1092

Sam's Oyster House
($$), 8495 Navarre Parkway
℗ 904/939-1998

Toby's Seafood Restaurant
($$), 8097 Navarre Parkway
℗ 904/939-5543

The Emerald Coast

Fort Walton Beach and **Destin**, its neighbour to the east, make up the Emerald Coast, which the locals describe as 'unpretentious, uncomplicated and breathtakingly beautiful', and it's easy to see why. The white-sand beaches run for 24 miles (38km) and most are protected from any development. There are also more than a hundred restaurants, over 10,000 beach rooms, ranging from seaside cottages to spacious condominiums and popular chain hotels, and six campsites.

The first settlers along this coast were Indians, and evidence of tribal ceremonies dating back to 500BC have been found among the dunes. The largest collection of prehistoric south-eastern Indian ceramics in the world – containing more than 6,000 pieces – is displayed at the Indian Temple Mound and Museum in Destin.

The first European visitor was the Spaniard Pánfilo de Narváez, who landed in 1528 in search of fresh water, but his landing party was sent packing by the Indians. In the second half of the eighteenth century, the area was controlled by infamous pirates such as Augustus Bowles, better known as 'Billy Bowlegs'. In 1778 Bowlegs formed the State of Muskogee, which stretched along the Emerald Coast in defiance of the Spanish, English and American authorities. There are, of course, countless tales of treasure buried along the coast.

The Emerald Coast became fashionable during the Prohibition era, when Chicago gangsters such as Al Capone built grand 'getaway' homes overlooking the Gulf and casinos to keep themselves entertained.

The stunning beaches and clear waters were chosen as the location for the film *Jaws II*, and although big fish are regularly caught here, the inshore waters are perfectly safe for family holidays. There are a number of seaside parks with pavilions, gazebos and facilities for the disabled to cross the dunes to the beaches. These include Henderson Beach State Park and Wayside and James Lee county parks.

The beaches are also one of the world's top locations for shell-collecting – queen helmet shells weighing more than 8lb (4kg) have been found here. Offshore, Sand Dollar City, a pure white sand-bar, and other ribboning reefs are rich with perfect shells. The waters also offer excellent diving among giant rays and sea turtles, while Timber Hole, a submerged petrified forest, also has a rich marine life. Even the dolphins put on a display as they play in the shallows close to shore. Those keen on fishing will be interested to learn that Destin claims to be the 'world's luckiest fishing village', and boasts five saltwater world records. The deep-sea fishing is outstanding because you can be in 100 fathoms (180m) of water only 10 miles (16km) from shore, while the local inshore waters are known as the 'Billfish Capital of the World'.

Eating out is another of the great pleasures of the area, with eateries ranging from rickety shack bars that serve the freshest of oysters to sophisticated seafood restaurants. The local waters yield the largest variety of seafood anywhere in Florida except the Keys, and you can enjoy red snapper, amberjack, yellowfin tuna and triggerfish brought straight in to the Destin harbour docks by the largest charter-boat fleet in the state. Try authentic Louisiana Cajun crawfish gumbo or beer-battered fried mullet.

Fort Walton Beach and Destin host many special events each

year, including Spring Splash, the Emerald Coast Golf Tournaments, Fort Walton Beach Seafood Festival, Destin Mayfest, Billy Bowlegs Festival, Hog's Breath Hobie Regatta, King Mackerel Tournament and other fishing tournaments, Eglin Air Show and the Christmas Boat Parade.

Emerald Coast Sights

Destin Bridge (at the Eglin Air Force Base; see below) is a 150-acre (60-hectare) reserve forming just part of the thousands of hectares of undisturbed wildlife preserve around the base. It is reached from Destin by taking Highway 98 over the bridge to Okaloosa Island. The beaches and sand flats provide nesting sites for terns and plovers between May and August, and many other species of gulls, waders, herons and egrets can be seen, as well as pelicans. Bottlenose dolphins can also be spotted in the inlet throughout the year.

Eglin Air Force Base (to the north of Destin) is home to the world's biggest environmental test chamber, which can create climatic conditions ranging from scorching temperatures to freezing blizzards. There are tours of the base. ℗ 904/882-3933

The **Focus Center** (Brooks Street) is a child's fantasy hands-on museum. Open: daily 1pm–5pm. ℗ 904/664-1261

The **Gulfarium** (Miracle Strip Parkway) features an exhibition called 'The Living Sea', as well as fourteen others housing seals, penguins, dolphins and scores of species of rainbow-coloured tropical fish. Open: daily, 9am–dusk, but call for details of show-times as these vary. ℗ 904/244-5169

The **Indian Temple Mound and Museum** (Miracle Strip Parkway) takes you on a journey spanning 10,000 years in the history of four tribes. It features the largest Indian temple mound ever discovered alongside salt water, this dating from AD1400. Open: daily. ℗ 904/243-6521

Old Destin Post Office Museum (Stahlman Avenue). A small local history museum housed in the old post office, opposite the library. Open: Wednesday 1.30pm 4.30pm. ℗ 904/837-8572.

The **US Air Force Armament Museum** (Highway 58) has displays spanning four wars. The twenty-five aircraft on show include the 'Blackbird' spy plane. Open: daily 9.30am–4.30pm. ℗ 904/882-4189

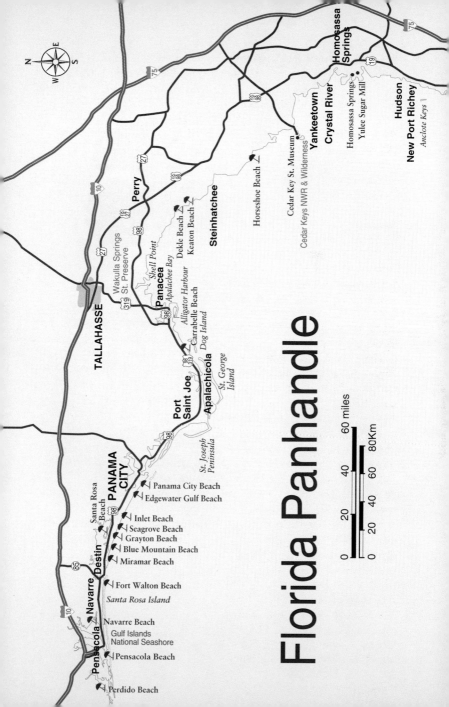

Emerald Coast Restaurants

(several of these are small seafood cafes with no telephone)

Back Porch
($$; home of chargrilled amberjack. Eat in or on picnic tables outside), Route 98
© 904/837-2022

Buster's Seafood and Oyster Bar
($$; Great restaurant which has served more than two million oysters. Try the toasted sea spider sandwich and marinated seagull legs), Route 98

Crab Trap
($$; Sensational seafood and pure Southern hospitality), James Lee Country Park

Fudpuckers
($$; Fun restaurants with great seafood and American family dining), Okaloosa Island and Destin.

Harbor Docks
($$; Three thatched tiki bars overlooking the docks and full of antiques. Try the seafood specialities and Annie's home made pies), Destin Docks

Harry T's
($$; A very unusual eatery run by circus trapeze artist Flying Harry T, containing Big Top and other eccentric exhibits ranging from a stuffed giraffe to treasures from the sunken luxury liner *Thracia*), Route 98

Hoser's,
($$; Eat surrounded by fire fighting memorabilia. The Three Alarm Chili is a spicey secret concoction topped with cheese and jalapenos and if one of the eighty imported beers cannot douse the flaming taste buds, the hose pipes on the wall might), Route 98

Louisiana Lagniappe
($$; A great Cajun restaurant. Try the seafood Lagniappe, pan cooked grouper topped with lobster medallions and smothered in garlic beurre blanc and hollandaise sauce), Holiday Inn, Sandpiper Cove

Marina Cafe
($$-$$$;Elegant candlelit, waterside dining with Italian and Louisianne influences. Try the baby escargot, Norwegian salmon or fettucini with andouille sausage, baby shrimp and spiced crawfish tails), Destin Dock

Sam's Oyster House
($$; The place for crab cracker, oyster shucking, giant shrimp and clams), Choctawhatchee Bay

Scampi's
($$; Built from the pilings of the original Destin Bridge.
Enormous seafood buffets
℡ 904/837-7686

Staff's
($$-$$$; The first restaurant on the coast and still going strong in a 1913 barrel shaped warehouse with pressed tin ceiling. Try the seafood skillet with the yellowfin tuna, shrimp, scallops and crabmeat stuffing, boiled in butter and dripping with cheese. It is served with baskets of home made wheat bread fresh-baked), Miracle Strip Parkway
℡ 904/243-3482

Beaches of South Walton

The next 26 miles (42km) of coastline are known as the **Beaches of South Walton**, but they are unlike most beaches you will have encountered. The shoreline consists of 40ft (12m-high) dunes and a vegetation and wildlife that has hardly been touched by man, plus mile after mile of white sands lapped by turquoise waters. Altogether there are eighteen pristine beaches along this stretch of coast; Grayton Beach was named the best beach in the nation out of 650 US beaches surveyed by Dr Stephen Leatherman.

At the east end of the Beaches of South Walton is the town of Seaside, while further west the Sandestin Resort, Seascape Resort, Tops'l Beach and Racquet Club all offer up-market accommodation. There are also quaint beachside cottages, cozy bed and breakfasts and campsites. Wonderful turn-of-the-century houses in the Panhandle architectural style are set amid beautiful grounds, such as the Eden State Gardens and Wesley Mansion in Point Washington, one of the first towns established in the area.

Remnants of the old town of Santa Rosa and its inhabitants' lifestyle can be found at the lookout point at Bayou Arts and Antiques on Hogtown Bayou in Santa Rosa Beach. Scenic Country Road 30A , which runs next to Seaside Beach, is noted for its antique shops, while artists' colonies can be found along the whole length of the Beaches of South Walton.

The area also boasts at least thirty-five restaurants offering fine dining and ranging in style from Cajun to Mediterranean and true Southern cooking. The award-winning Criolla's Restaurant features Creole-Caribbean cuisine at its best, while other recommended eateries include Sandestin Resort's Elephant Walk Restaurant, La Pergola in Blue Mountain Beach and Bud and Alley's in Seaside, whose dishes are seasoned with home-grown herbs.

The unspoiled beaches and hinterland offer great bird-watching, hiking and nature trails. Fishing, both fresh- and saltwater, is also popular. Freshwater catches include bass, bream and catfish, while fishing in Choctawhatchee Bay yields red fish, speckled trout and flounder. Saltwater catches include flounder, grouper, sailfish, marlin, amberjack, barracuda, cobia, tarpon and many other species. Boat and fishing charters are available, while at the ninety-eight-slip Baytowne Marina at Sandestin you can also hire hobie cats, waverunners, jet-skis, pontoon boats and other small craft.

Back on land, there are seven local golf courses and plenty of opportunities to play tennis. There are bike rentals at Sandestin Bicycle Rental (Sandestin Resort), Seaside Bicycle Rental (Savannah Street, Seaside) and Sea-grove Villas Bicycle Rental (just west of Seaside on Country Road 30A).

Popular shopping spots include The Market at Sandestin, Seaside town centre and Ruskin Place, the Gallery at Grayton, the World's Tiniest Gallery (Magnolia Street, Grayton Beach), Silver Sands' factory stores, South Walton's antique shops, and Emerald Coast Plaza, Delchamp's Plaza and Beach Walk Center in South Walton.

Beaches of South Walton Sights

Cassine Garden's Nature Trail (behind the Cassine Garden townhouses on County Road 30A) is a nature trail and boardwalk that meanders for 3 miles (5km) through scenic marshlands and forests and across white-sand beaches. A 1mile (1.6km) fitness trail is incorporated along the way. The trail is not lit but is always open. Admission is free. ✆ 904/231-5721

Eden State Gardens and the Wesley Mansion (at Point Washington on County Road 395 off Highway 98) is a turn-of-the-century mansion set in landscaped gardens. The gardens are open daily 8am–sundown and there are guided tours of the mansion on the hour 9am–4pm. Admission to the park is free but there is a charge for the tours. ✆ 904/231-4214

Historic **Grayton Beach** is one of the oldest communities on the north-western coast and has many fine old buildings along its sandy, tree-lined streets. The Washaway House was built in the early 1900s by Civil War veteran General William Miller, one of the original homesteaders.

Grayton Beach State Recreation Area offers self-guided trails through the special dune ecosystem. Open: daily 8am–sundown. Admission is charged per vehicle. ✆ 904/231-4210

Above: *The Emerald Coast Gulfarium* **Below:** *Destin*

Panama City Beach

The award-winning **Panama City Beach** is the next stop along the coast. It stretches for 27 miles (45km) and has emerald-green waters and white quartz sand. In 1995 one of the nearby beaches, St Andrews Recreation Area, was voted the best beach in the US, while Panama City Beach itself was voted the third-best sports beach in the nation, ideal for swimming, fishing, windsurfing, boating, sailing, jet-skiing, parasailing, diving and snorkelling. St Andrews Recreation Area has jetties that extend almost a 0.5 mile (1km) into the Gulf for fishermen and sightseers, and a shuttle boat crosses to the aptly named Shell Island at the entrance to St Andrew's Bay. The waters here are rich in fish thanks to the Yucatan current, which carries the food nutrients for blue marlin, sailfish, bull dolphin (the fish), wahoo and tuna. St Andrew's Bay also offers good diving, with clear waters, numerous shipwrecks and fifty artificial reefs.

Land-based activities include golf, tennis, miniature golf and greyhound racing at Ebro Greyhound Park. This is a true family destination and is becoming increasingly popular with international visitors, who can fly into the recently expanded Panama City/Bay County International Airport.

Panama City Beach also claims to be the 'Seafood Capital of the World', and has a wealth of excellent restaurants to suit all tastes and pockets. The area has more than 18,000 rooms in hotels, motels and condominiums, as well as campsites, RV parks and rental homes.

Panama City Beach Sights

Bay County's Junior Museum (Jenks Avenue) is a hands-on participation hall with science, art and nature exhibits.

Gran Maze (off State Road 98) is as large as a football field and the first maze of its kind in the US.

Gulf World (Front Beach Road) is a marine park with animals, birds and aquariums set in tropical gardens. There are shows and demonstrations. Open: daily from 9am. ℰ 904/234-5271

Miracle Strip Amusement Park (Highway 98A) has thirty rides, including one of the world's most exciting roller-coasters.

Museum of Man in the Sea (Back Beach Road) is the only museum in the world devoted solely to the history of diving. There are some 1,500 exhibits on display. Open: daily 9am–5pm. ℰ 904/235-4101

Ocean Opry Show (Front Beach Road) is a 1,000-seat family-orientated theatre featuring a wide range of music. Open: every evening. ℰ 904/234-5464

Shipwreck Island (Front Beach Road) has six landscaped acres with thirty slides, rides and attractions, plus picnic areas and lots of water. The adventurous seek out the Rapid River's Cascade or the 370 feet White Water tube. ℭ 904/234-0368

Panama City Beach Restaurants

All American Diner
($-$$; Open all day for buffet dining). 10590 Front Beach Road
ℭ 850/235-2443

Angelo's Steak Pit
($$; Great steaks and ribs but open for dinner only).
9527 Front Beach Road
ℭ 904/234-2531

Bayview Restaurant
($$; Open all day for seafood and American dishes)
4200 Marriott Drive
ℭ 904/234-3307

Beach BBQ
($-$$; Open all day for fast food and grills), 2920 Thomas Drive,
ℭ 904/233-7727

Billy's Oyster Bar
($$ Oyster and fish bar open for lunch and dinner),
3000,Thomas Drive
ℭ 850/235-2349

Bishop's Family Buffet
($-$$; Open all day with great value buffet speads),

12628 Front Beach Road
ℭ 904/234-6457

Boar's Head Restaurant
($$; American menu with seafood specialities, open for dinner only),
17290 Front Beach Road
ℭ 904/234-6628

Cajun Inn
($$; Great Cajun and seafood specialities), 477 Beckrich Road,
ℭ 850/235-9987

Charlie's Restaurant
($$ American)
12386 Front Beach Road.
ℭ 850/235-3976

Chicago Dawg
($-$$; American fast food eatery, open all day),
10812 Front Beach Road
ℭ 850/235-2800

Dusty's Oyster Bar
($$; Waterfront, oysterbar)
16450 Front Beach Road
ℭ 904/233-0035

House of Thailand
($$; Elegant Thai restaurant on the waterfront),
16010 Front Beach Road
ℭ 904/234-9703

Sunset Grill and Pub
($$;On the waterfront and open all day for American dishes and steaks),
100 Delwood Boulevard
ℭ 850/235-6909

East to Apalachicola

Tyndall Air Force Base, 10 miles (16km) east of Panama City on Highway 98, is situated on a 29,000-acre (11,600-hectare) peninsula which juts out into the Gulf, and although it is occupied by the military there are opportunities for the public to bird-watch, collect shells, fish and swim (stop at the visitor's checkpoint for a pass). Warbler's Way is a short elevated boardwalk that runs through the freshwater marsh to an observation tower. There are the 1mile (1.6km) Deer Run Nature Trail and many tidal pools to explore. The access to East End Beach is 1 mile west of Mexico Beach on Highway 98.

After Mexico Beach and St Joe Beach, the next main town along the highway is **Port Saint Joe**. Apart from its beaches, the town's top attraction is the **Constitution Convention State Museum** on Highway 98, which preserves the site of the state's first constitutional convention. There are also exhibits on local history. Open: Thursday to Monday 9am–noon and 1pm–5pm. ✆ 904/229-8029

The **St Joseph Peninsula State Park** lies south of Port St Joe. Take Highway 98 for about 1.5 miles (2.4km) and then Country Road 30A for about 6 miles (9km). Turn west onto Country Road 30E and continue for a further 8 miles (13km) to reach the park entrance. Apart from a rich collection of wildlife, the park has miles of white-sand beaches along a sand spit which runs parallel to the coast. The area teems with birdlife, both migrating and nesting, and with migrating butterflies in the autumn. This is also the best place in Florida to see peregrine falcons. The northern part of the park is a designated wilderness preserve where only hiking and primitive camping are allowed. The rest of the park offers good fishing, swimming and camping, while skunks and raccoons are regular evening visitors to the campsites.

To the south is the Bay of San Blas, and from here the road runs south-east across St Vincent Sound to **Apalachicola**, famous for its oyster beds. The small town is named after the Hitchiti Indian word for 'people on the other side'. About ninety per cent of the state's oysters are farmed in the town's 10,000 acres (4,000 hectares) of oyster beds, and the bivalves are the main feature of the town's annual Florida Seafood Festival in November. Local attractions include the **John Gorrie State Museum** (6th Street and Avenue D), which has local history exhibits and displays on the life and inventions of Dr Gorrie, the man responsible for ice machines, refrigeration and air-conditioning. Open: Thursday to Monday 9am–noon and 1pm–5pm. ✆ 904/653-9347

Above: *The Carrebelle River* **Below:** *San Marcos de Apalache State Historical Site*

The **Apalachicola National Forest**, to the north, covers more than 500,000 acres (200,000 hectares) and can be viewed along the 30mile (50km) Apalachee Savannah Scenic Byway. The forest, consisting of long-leaf pine, cypress swamps and prairie savannah, has many rare plant communities and spectacular wildflower displays, as well as more colonies of the endangered red cockaded woodpecker than anywhere else in the world. It is also a good place to spot other woodpeckers, warblers and both swallow-tailed and Mississippi kites, as well as white-tailed deer, squirrels and wild turkeys.

Tallahassee

The state capital, **Tallahassee**, lies to the north-east of the Apalachicola National Forest, and while not on the coast, this intimate, historic city is worth a visit. It was an Indian tribal centre long before the first Europeans, under Spanish conquistador Hernando de Soto, established a winter camp here in 1539.

The city nestles in the foothills of the Appalachian Mountains at the junction of Florida's Panhandle and peninsula, in the area known as Big Bend. This is a region of lush rolling hills dotted with plantations, towering pines, cypresses, snowy dogwoods, fragrant magnolias and hundreds of shimmering lakes, springs, rivers, ponds, swamps and sink holes. There are five 'official' canopy roads – Old St Augustine, Miccosukee, Meridian, Centreville and Old Bainbridge – which travel through fantastic tunnels of ancient moss-draped live oaks. Around the city there are six private and public golf courses, tennis courts, cycle and hiking tracks, and fishing and boating on lakes Jackson, Talquin, Iamonia and Miccosukee.

Tallahassee itself has many attractions, wonderful old buildings and fine arts venues. The latter include the Florida State Dance Repertory Theater, the Tallahassee Symphony Orchestra, the Monticello Opera House, the Florida State School of Music, the Orchesis Contemporary Dance Theater and the Tallahassee Ballet Company, as well as several theatres. The city and area offer 5,000 rooms in fifty-six hotels and motels, fifteen campsites, and attracts more than 2 million visitors a year. The many memorable restaurants serve a host of local specialities, such as fresh fried mullet, Bradley's country sausage, Whigham pecans (deep fried and rolled in cinnamon sugar), Cairo pickles, Mama Crum's blackened seafood seasoning and Blackberry Patch jams. The locally grown sweet vidalia onions are eaten like a piece of fruit, while Quincy mushrooms and Jefferson County watermelons are equally famous.

Recommended restaurants include the up-market and prestigious Andrew's Second Act.

The Old Town Trolley provides free transportation through downtown, and the tourist information centre offers a number of free brochures on things to do, including easy-to-follow self-guided walking tours around the Park Avenue and Calhoun Street Historic Districts. Finally, there is excellent shopping in Governor's Square, Tallahassee Mall, Parkway Center and Village Commons.

Tallahassee Sights

Adams Street Commons is surrounded by historic brick buildings that now house eateries and interesting shops. ✆ 904/224-3252

Governor's Mansion is modelled on Andrew Jackson's colonnaded home, the Hermitage. The Georgian-style mansion was built in 1956 and is furnished with eighteenth and nineteenth-century collectibles. The grounds are noted for their giant magnolia trees. Open for tours only. ✆ 904/488-4661

The **Museum of Florida History** traces the history of the region from prehistoric times to the present day. Open: Monday to Friday 9am–4.30pm, Saturday 10am–4.30pm and Sunday noon–4.30pm. ✆ 904/488-1484

New Capitol is worth visiting, especially for its twenty-second-floor observatory which offers views all the way to the Gulf. Open: Monday to Friday 8am–5pm and weekends 8.30am–4.30pm. ✆ 904/413-9200

Old Capitol has been restored to its 1902 American Renaissance appearance, with red candy-striped awnings and a glorious dome, the so-called 'pearl' of Capitol Hill. Open: Monday to Friday 9am–4.30pm, Saturday 10am–4.30pm and Sunday noon–4.30pm. ✆ 904/487-1902.

The **Tallahassee Museum of History and Natural Science** is set in 52 acres (20 hectares) of grounds. Open: Monday to Saturday 9am–5pm and Sunday 12.30pm–5pm. ✆ 904/576-1636

The **Vietnam Veteran's Memorial** faces the Old Capitol. The 12m (40ft) twin granite towers honour Florida's casualties; the huge American flag suspended in their honour was dedicated in 1985. Open: permanently accessible.

Tallahassee Natural Attractions

Natural attractions in the city include the Alfred B Maclay State Gardens, created by the New York financier in the grounds of his home; Killearn Gardens on the banks of Lake Hall (open: 8am–sunset; Prime Meridian Marker in the heart of town; and the Florida National Scenic Trail, a hiking trail which offers a glimpse of the original Florida.

Opposite: *The old and new capitol, Tallahassee*
Above: *Pensacola Beach* ***Below:*** *Sponges, Pinellas Suncoast*

Tallahassee Historical Sights

The **Brokaw-McDougall House** (1856) has six magnificent imported Corinthian columns, and is a mix of Classical Revival and Italian architecture. Open: Monday to Friday 8am–5pm. ✆ 904/488-3901

The Columns was built in 1830 'with a nickel in every brick'. The white colonnaded mansion is Tallahassee's oldest-surviving home. Open: Monday to Thursday 8am–5.30pm and Friday 8am–5pm. ✆ 904/224-8116

The **De Soto Archaeological and Historic Site** was the spot where, in 1539, Hernando de Soto and his Spanish soldiers celebrated the first Christmas in North America. Copper coins found at the site are the oldest unearthed in the US. Open: sunrise–sunset. ✆ 850/922-6007

The **First Presbyterian Church** was built in 1838 and is the oldest church in the city. It welcomed slaves as independent members without their masters' consent.

Lake Jackson State Archaeological Site is the sacred burial ground of Florida's Lake Jackson Indians. Guided tours and interpretative programmes are available. Open: sunrise–sunset. ✆ 904/562-0042

Natural Bridge Battlefield State Historic Site is the scene of the area's only Civil War battle, fought on 6 March 1865, when the Confederates forced the Union troops to retreat to St Marks Lighthouse where they had landed only a few hours earlier. ✆ 904/925-6216

San Luis Archaeological and Historic Site is a seventeenth-century Spanish mansion and Indian settlement that was created 200 years before Florida became a state. Open: Monday to Friday 9am–4.30pm, Saturday 10am–4pm and Sunday noon–4.30pm. ✆ 904/487-3711

San Marcos de Apalache (to the south of Tallahassee) was built in 1679 to protect Spanish missionaries. ✆ 904/925-6216

Union Bank (down the hill from the Capitol Complex) was built in 1841 and is Florida's oldest-surviving bank. Open: Tuesday to Friday 10am–1pm and weekends 1pm–4pm. ✆ 904/487-3803

Tallahassee Restaurants

**Andrew's Upstairs
and Andrew's Second Act**
S Adams Street
Chez Pierre
N Adams Street

Goodies Eatery
E College Avenue

Grand Central Café
W College Avenue

Maggie May's Café
S Calhoun Street

Panini's
E College Avenue

Po Boys Creole Café
E College Avenue

220 Club
S Monroe Street

Uptown Café
E College Avenue

Back to the Coast

The **Wakulla Springs State Park** lies to the south of Tallahassee and is reached on Highway 319 or 61. About 2 miles (3km) past Capitol Circle, turn left onto Highway 61 and continue for just over 7 miles (11km) to Highway 267. Turn left here and then immediately right to reach the park entrance. The park covers some 2,860 acres (1,144 hectares), and offers nature trails and ranger-led river cruises in glass-bottomed boats. Wakulla Springs itself is one of the world's largest and deepest freshwater springs, while the Wakulla River runs through the park's old cypress swamps and woodlands. The park is also a popular swimming and snorkelling area, and in addition to a wealth of birdlife there are gators, turtles, snakes and white-tailed deer. Open: daily. © 904/922-3632

Alligator Point, west along the coast, is a natural-dune public beach with no facilities, although accommodation, campsites, restaurants, fuel and groceries are available in the nearby fishing villages. **St George Island**, reached via a causeway, is a pristine 29 miles (47km) long barrier island beach that is ideal for swimming, shelling, boating and fishing, and has a campsite, RV and picnic facilities, and toilets and showers in the St George Island State Park. The park is rich in birdlife, especially nesting waders and shore birds, and loggerhead turtles nest on the beach during the summer months. Open: 8am–sunset. © 904/927-2111.

Back on the mainland, **Carrabelle** offers swimming, shelling, toilets and picnic tables with shelters, although the sand is more coarse here than further west. **Dog Island**, facing Carrabelle, has a pristine sandy beach that is accessible only by boat or plane. There are charters and ferries from Carrabelle but there are no public facilities on the island. **Marshes Sands Beach** has shallow water for swimming, shelling and crabbing. There are toilets and showers, picnic tables, shelters, grills and a snack bar. Posey's Motel offers accommodation and a restaurant, and there is a campsite, fuel and grocery stores near by.

Further east along the coast is **Shell Point** noted mostly for watersports, especially sailing and windsurfing. Shell Point Resort offers accommodation, dining, a marina and boat charters. There is fishing and golf near by. **Panacea** is known as the 'Blue Crab Capital of the World'. Its annual crab festival attracts about 20,000 people every year.

St Marks National Wildlife Refuge covers 65,000 acres (26,000 hectares) of salt marshes, pine flats and oak uplands along Apalachee Bay, accessible via plenty of hiking and bicycle trails. The entrance to the refuge is on County Road 59 off Highway 98. Apart from a rich birdlife in the pools and along the beach, you can spot gators, bobcats, otters and white-tailed deer. Many species of wildflowers grow around the historic St Mark's lighthouse, and the refuge plays hosts to thousands of butterflies during their autumn passage.

The Big Bend

The beaches around Big Bend do not compare with those further west, but there are a number of places worth visiting.

Hickory Mound Impoundment, an artificial enclosure created to form a wetland habitat, is encircled by a 6.5 miles (10.5km) dike and covers 1,834 acres (734 hectares) on the Gulf. It is reached from Highway 98 along Cow Creek Road. You can drive or walk along the levee to look at the many waders, ducks and overwintering geese and swans. Many species of birds of prey can also be seen.

Hagen's Cove is also part of the Big Bend Wildlife Management Area and has some wonderful undisturbed beaches. Take Highway 27a south from **Perry** for about 4.5 miles (7km) and then turn right onto County Road 361. Continue for a further 22 miles (35km) to Hagen's Cove Road, turning right to reach the parking area. There are fine views of the pine islands and shallow bays of the Gulf from the observation tower south of the parking area, and there is also a boat ramp. Good beaches in the area include **Dekle Beach** and **Keaton Beach**, while there is good boating and fishing from **Steinhatchee**.

The main highway then continues south, with the turn-off to Highway 351 leading to the coast and **Horseshoe Beach**. Once past Manatee Springs State Park on the Suwannee River, take Highway 24 for the beaches of Cedar Key, the next port of call along the coast.

The **Cedar Keys** are a group of islands lying about 15 miles (24km) south of the mouth of the Suwannee River. **Cedar Key** itself is a small, pretty fishing village surrounded by salt marshes, sand-pine scrub, pine flats and scores of tidal

Opposite: Sponge diver, Tarpon Springs

creeks. During the Civil War, the village was used by blockage runners to export cotton and timber, which was sold to buy food and supplies for the Confederacy. After the war, timber, then fishing and ship-building were the main industries. In 1896 the town was literally flattened by a hurricane, and the small community that emerged is now mainly concerned with tourism and commercial fishing, including crabbing and oyster farming. It is also the home of a flourishing artists' colony, the Sidewalk Festival in April giving them the chance to showcase their work. A seafood festival is also held in the third week of October.

There are self-guided tours of the town, while the **Cedar Key Historical Society Museum** (State Road 24) relates the history of the area back to Indian times. Open: daily 11am–4pm. © 352/543-5549. The **Cedar Key State Museum** (signposted north of State Road 24) displays old household artefacts, historical dioramas and the shell collection of St Clair Williams, said to be one of the most complete ever assembled. Open: Thursday to Monday 9am–5pm. © 352/543-5350

The Cedar Key islands are also home to thousands of birds, while alongside the road you can usually spot scrub jays and the burrows of gopher tortoises. There is a good beach at Yankeetown, south along the mainland.

Cedar Key Restaurants

The Brown Pelican
($$; Overlooking the water with local seafood, pasta and a la carte menu with children's dishes), Cedar Cove Beach and Yacht Club
© 352/543-6520

Heron Restaurant
($$; Casual a la carte dining in an old Victorian building), Junction of 2nd Street and State Road 24
© 352/543-5666.

Crystal River to Tarpon Springs

Crystal River is a National Historic Landmark, an area of great archaeological interest and one of the oldest and longest-inhabited Indian sites in Florida. Excavations have revealed settlements dating back to prehistoric times and signs of a remarkably advanced civilization; one grave contained a complicated astronomical calendar. The six-mound complex over 14 acres (5 hectares) and was the home of a group known as the pre-Columbian mound-builders. The site was an important ceremonial and burial centre for 1,600 years, and as many as 7,500

Native Americans are thought to have visited it annually, often travelling long distances to trade or to bury their dead. There is a small museum at the Crystal River Archaeological Site containing Indian artefacts dating back to 150BC. From the highest temple mound there are views across the river. Crystal River is also noted for the large number of manatees that congregate there, these being attracted by the local warm springs, especially in winter.

The coastline around Cedar Key is quite marshy and there arc no fine beaches, but you should visit the famous **Homosassa Springs State Wildlife Park**. It covers 155 acres (62 hectares) and is dominated by the massive crystal-clear Spring of Ten Thousand Fish, which has a year-round temperature of 72°F (22°C). The spring is unusual in that it is home to about thiry-five species of both freshwater and saltwater species of fish, as well as manatees. You can descend into the observation room, where large windows allow you to view the teeming fish life in the 45ft (14m) deep spring. The entrance to the park is on Highway 19 in Homosassa Springs. Also to be seen here are a wide variety of Florida birds, gators, black bears, turtles, bobcats, river otters and white-tailed deer, and there are boat trips along Pepper Creek, a spring-fed stream which runs into the Homosassa River.

You can watch alligators being fed at Gator Lagoon, while the Animal Encounters Arena features Floridian snakes and other local wildlife and holds educational programmes focusing on the manatee and alligator. There are walking trails and boat trips at the latter, and there is also a manatee rehabilitation facility where the injured mammals can be treated. Open: daily 9am–5.30pm.
℡ 352/628-5343

The **Yulee Sugar Mill Ruins State Historic Site** is situated on State Road 490, west of Highway 19 in Homosassa. The 5,100 acre (2,040 hectare) park was once part of a prosperous sugar plantation owned by David Levy Yulee, Florida's first US senator, who employed 1,000 slaves there. The mill was built in 1851 and operated for thirteen years, supplying sugar to Confederate troops during the Civil War. There are picnic facilities. Open: daily 8am–dusk. ℡ 352/795-3817.

Marshes along the next stretch of coastline make up another national wildlife refuge, this one including **Pine Island**, with its fine beach, and Raccoon Point. The next stop on the journey south is the world-famous **Weeki Wachee Springs**, a combined theme and nature park built around some of the many natural springs found in the area. The main spring flows at the rate of 170 million gallons (770 million litres) a day and the

temperature is a constant 74°F (23°C). The attraction is most famous for its 'mermaids', who put on several acrobatic-ballet shows a day in the unique underwater theatre. There are also shows featuring exotic birds and birds of prey. The 'Wilderness' river cruises explore typical Floridian fauna and flora and include a stop at the pelican reserve. A large number of animals are on display, there is a petting zoo and there is also a rehabilitation centre for injured seabirds. Open: daily 9.30am–5.30pm (closing times vary according to season). ✆ 352/596-2062.

Buccanneer Bay, next door, is a water park centred on another natural spring but also has a white-sand beach. There are water slides, river rides, a children's play area, eateries, lockers, toilets and picnic areas. Open: daily 10am–5pm (later in the summer). ✆ 352/596-2062.

To the south of Weeki Wachee lies Hernando Beach, beyond which you cross over into Pasco County and head down to the sprawling conurbation of Clearwater, St Petersburg and the surrounding city suburbs. Pasco County has more than 20 miles (32km) of Gulf Coast frontage, and has undergone major development in the last few years as many of its communities have

Opposite: The Tarpon Springs fishing fleet

attracted people looking for good weather and a relaxed way of life. As a result, cities such as Port Richey and its inland neighbour, New Port Richey, have expanded considerably.

The county is often called 'nature's playground' as so much land has been set aside for parks and recreation, including beaches, lakes and rivers, wilderness parks and recreation complexes. Campers can spend the night under the stars in wilderness parks which also have nature trails and picnic areas. There are good beaches at **Holiday**, **Hudson**, **Port Richey** and **Anclote**, and the entire strip of coastline offers excellent boating, diving, and fishing opportunites. There are canoe trips and excellent fresh-water fishing inland, plus a host of other outdoor activities, from golf (with more than a score of courses to choose from) and tennis to horseback riding and skydiving.

Anclote River Park offers a 7 miles (11km) motor tour along the mangrove coastline, the mouth of the Anclote River and Gulf beaches. The loop trail starts by taking Country Road 595A off Highway 19 south of New Port Richey. Follow 595A (also known as Baileys Bluff Road) to North Anclote River Park, south past the power station to South Anclote River Park, and then along Anclote Boulevard to connect with Alternate Highway 19. You can then either return north via Holiday to complete the loop, or continue south to Tarpon Springs.

The **Anclote Keys** lie 3 miles (5km) off Tarpon Springs and are accessible only by private charter boat. The 4 miles (6km) of beautiful Gulf coastline are dominated in the south by a federal lighthouse that was built in 1887. Besides swimming, the keys are ideal for nature-watching as they are divided into six separate fauna zones. Scores of bird species can be seen, including bald eagles, rare piping plovers and ospreys, the latter nesting in the tall pine trees found here. All water and food supplies have to be taken to the island, and all litter removed.

Tarpon Springs is known as the 'Sponge Capital of the World' and is Florida's 'Little Greece'. The Greek influence is very strong here as Greek fishermen and sponge divers helped settle the area in 1876. By the 1890s the town was a thriving port, and today there is still a Mediterranean atmosphere around the picturesque sponge dock. The sponge boats anchor along the quay, while the other side of the road is packed with shops that sell more sponges than you have ever seen, as well as Greek restaurants and bakeries. Although you get the impression of being in a coastal port, Tarpon Springs actually lies some way inland on the Anclote River.

Apart from sightseeing around the town, there are a number of cruises and fishing trips available. You can cruise down the Anclote River into the Gulf, ferry across to secluded Anclote Island at the mouth of the river and enjoy a day on its beaches, or go out to sea to watch a sponge diver at work. As you travel down to the river's wide estuary, you pass magnificent waterside homes and a charming little beach that has become popular as the water here is warmer due to the power station opposite.

Every year on Epiphany (6 January) the Greek Orthodox Church stages a procession through the streets, after which young men dive to retrieve a white cross which is thrown into the water. The one who finds it is said to be blessed with good luck for the coming year. The day also features Greek food, dancing and entertainment. Other major annual events include the Tarpon Spings Arts and Crafts Festival in April, the Not Just a Seafood Festival along the sponge docks in May, and the JC Penney Golf Classic at the Innisbrook Resort in December.

Tarpon Springs Sights

The **Konger Coral Sea Aquarium** (Dodecanese Boulevard) has a simulated coral reef and marine life in a 100,000-gallon (450,000-litre) tank, a tidal pool and a moray eel exhibit.

Open: daily 10am–5pm.
℃ 813/938-5378

The Spongeorama Exhibit Center (Dodecanese Boulevard) includes the Museum of Sponge Diving History. Open: daily 10am-5pm. Admission is free.
℃ 813/943-9509

Crystal River to Tarpon Springs Restaurants

Bill's Lighthouse Restaurant
($ American Seafood)
813 Dodecanese Blvd,
Tarpon Springs
℃ 813/938-4895

Dino's ($$ Greek),
604 Athens Street,
Tarpon Springs
℃ 813/938-9082

Leverocks, ($$; Overlooking the marina, American specialities),
4927 US 19 South
℃ 813/864-3883

Mama Maria's Greek Restaurant
($$; Lively traditional Greek taverna serving Greek dishes and seafood), 509 Athens Street,
Tarpon Springs
℃ 813/938-5475

Mykonos
($$ Greek)
628 Dodecanese Blvd,
Tarpon Springs
℃ 813/934-4306

Red Lobster, ($$ Sea food)
5711 US 19
New Port Richey
℃ 813/848-2211

Seaport Inn
($$; Seafood, steaks and oriental dishes to eat in or to take out),
11217 US 19
℃ 813/863-5402

Sam's Seafront Restaurant
($$ Seafood)
6325 Clark Street,
Hudson
℃ 813/868-1971

The French Quarter
($$; A la carte bistro-style dining serving traditional French fare),
200 East Tarpon Avenue,
Tarpon Springs
℃ 813/942-3011

Pinellas Suncoast

The Suncoast includes the eight communities of Palm Harbor, Dunedin, Largo, Clearwater Beach, St Petersburg, Indian Rocks Beach, Madeira Beach and Treasure Island. It is particularly famous for its 28 miles (45km) of snow-white sandy beaches and warm blue waters. Virtually every kind of water activity is catered for, from deep-sea fishing, sailing and windsurfing to parasailing, jet-skiing and diving. There are forty-three golf courses, more than sixty marinas and yacht

Above: The harbour, Tarpon Springs
Below: The Visitor Centre, Homosassa Springs

clubs, as well as shopping and dining opportunities galore. The area boasts more than 1,800 restaurants, with seafood dishes a speciality, and there are also romantic dinner cruises and dinner theatres. There are almost 500 hotels and motels offering nearly 20,000 rooms, more than 4,000 rental condominiums, thousands of private homes for rent, and scores of campsites and RV parks.

As you travel south down the coast, the Gulf beaches you pass are Crystal Beach and Palm Harbor, Honeymoon Island, Caladesi Island, Clearwater Beach, Bellair Beach, Bellair Shore, Indian Rocks Beach, Indian Shores, Redington Shores, North Redington Beach, Redington Beach, Madeira Beach, Treasure Island, St Pete's Beach and Fort DeSoto Park. Three of the area's beaches feature in the list of the finest in the US: Caladesi Island State Park in Dunedin, voted the second-best beach in the nation in 1995 (out of 650); Fort DeSoto Park in St Petersburg was rated eighth; and Sand Key Park in Clearwater was ranked twelfth. Clearwater Beach was also rated the best municipal beach along the entire Gulf Coast.

John Chestnut Senior County Park is a protected area of cypress swamps and pine flatwoods on the south-eastern shores of Lake Tarpon. There are many nature trails, boating and canoeing on Brooker Creek, and pretty picnic spots and playground facilities in abundance. You can spot turtles and gators sunning themselves by the water, and the observation platform offers a bird's-eye view of the park and its wildlife. The park is reached via Highway 19 in Palm Harbor by taking Tampa Road (Highway 584) east to East Lake Road and then driving north for about 2 miles (3km) to the entrance.

Honeymoon Island State Recreation Area is a typical Gulf Coast barrier island: long and thin with glorious white-sand beaches on the Gulf side and mangrove swamps on the bay side, and with pine forests and tidal flats between. Originally known as Hog Island, its name was changed in 1939 when a New York developer built fifty palm-thatched honeymoon bungalows here. There are magnificent beaches, safe swimming, good fishing and lots of wildlife to be seen from the nature trails that wind through the mangrove swamps and tidal flats. Accessed by the Dunedin Causeway, the island is another getaway-from-it-all location and is ideal for those who like shell-collecting. It lies 3 miles (5km) north of Dunedin off Highway 19, accessed via the causeway from Curlew Road (Highway 586). Open: daily 8am–sunset. ✆ 813/469-5942.

Award-winning **Caladesi Island**

State Park covers more than 1, 170 acres (468 hectares), and until 1848 was part of Hurricane Island to the north. That year a hurricane separated it, and the still undeveloped island is now only accessible by private boat or ferry from Honeymoon Island. It is worth making the short trip for the island's beautiful 5km (3 miles) of pristine beaches and for its shoreline walks. It is one of the state's few remaining undisturbed barrier islands, and is ideal for swimming, shell-collecting, picnics, skin- and scuba-diving, and nature study. Off shore you can spot bottlenose dolphins, while on the beach you may see the trails of loggerhead turtles which come ashore here to lay their eggs. Inland there are gopher tortoises, raccoons, snakes and large numbers of birds. There are many unspoiled island trails. There is a small marina and offshore anchorage for boats between March and Labor Day (beginning of September); overnight visitors must register before sundown.

Dunedin lies north of Clearwater and was founded by Scottish settlers in 1870. There are two state parks here that are ideal for peaceful days out by the beach. Alternatively, you can take a ferry from Honeymoon Island to Caladesi Island (see above) to see what life was like when the coastline was being explored by the Spanish in the 1500s. The area's Scottish heritage is vividly born out every year by the local Highland games, held in spring.

Things to see include the **Dunedin Fine Art Centre** (Michigan Boulevard), which has a small fine art collection and exhibits work by local artists. Open: Monday to Friday 9am–5pm and Sunday 1pm–4pm (closed Saturday). ℂ 813/738 1892. The **Dunedin Historical Museum** (Main Street) was originally the 1889 railroad station for the Orange Belt railroad system. It now displays drawings and relics from this Scottish community's past, and also organizes walking tours of the town's historic areas. Open: Tuesday to Saturday 10am–1pm. ℂ 813/733-4151.

To reach the **Upper Tampa Bay County Park**, drive south-east of Oldsmar on Highway 580, and then south on Double Branch Road to the park entrance. The park shows how the region's coastal wetlands looked before development took hold, and has salt marshes, mangroves, pine hammocks and salt flats along Old Tampa Bay and Double Branch Creek. This is a great area for canoeing and wildlife-watching. The Nature Center gives an excellent overview of the park's history and wildlife, and nature trails follow boardwalks through some of the park's otherwise inaccessible marshes.

Safety Harbor lies on the north shore of Tampa Bay and has many impressive waterside homes, most of which have their own boat docks. **Philippe Park** (Bayshore Drive) is named after Count Odet Philippe, a surgeon under Napoleon who settled the site in the 1830s and introduced the first grapefruit trees to the New World. Before his arrival, it was used as an Indian settlement and as a base for Spanish exploration. A large ceremonial Indian mound can still be seen in the park. ✆ 813/726-2700. **Safety Harbor Museum of Regional History** (South Bayshore Boulevard) traces the area's history and houses many early Indian artefacts. Open: Tuesday to Friday 10am–4pm, and weekends 1pm–4pm. ✆ 813/726-1668.

Weedon Island State Preserve lies just off the western shore of Old Tampa Bay south of Gandy Bridge. A former 1,000 acre (400 hectare) citrus grove, the park is now one of the few remaining mangrove swamps and green spaces in Florida's most densely populated county. In the 1920s, the citrus grove was uprooted and the island became home to a roaring 1920s nightclub, a motion picture studio and one of Florida's first airports. During this development, one of Florida's most important archaeological finds was unearthed, providing evidence of settlement dating back to AD300. Today, the park offers a wealth of wildlife, plus opportunities for hiking, canoeing, fishing and picnicking.

St Petersburg and Clearwater

St Petersburg and Clearwater occupy the Pinellas Peninsula in Pinellas County. The name Pinellas means 'Point of Pines', and was chosen by Spanish explorers in the early 1500s. The two cities and the surrounding communities and suburbs together make up the most densely populated area in all Florida.

St Petersburg and Clearwater make ideal bases for holidays, especially for those looking for a relaxed vacation near the water. The Gulf is warm and safe to swim in, and the sandy beaches are ideal for lazing on and for sunbathing. But the area offers a lot more than sun, sea and sand. There are sophisticated shops, cultural events and activities, a galaxy of sporting opportunities, attractions and entertainments, and numerous excellent restaurants.

The St Petersburg-Clearwater International Airport is serviced by a growing number of international charters. The airport is linked to the interstate highway system and accessible from Interstate 75, Interstate 275 and Interstate 4. Some beach areas are serviced by trolley cars. Public transportation throughout Pinellas County is

Opposite: Queuing for fish, Clearwater **Above:** Clearwater Beach
Below: View from the bridge, John's Pass

provided by the Pinellas Suncoast Transit Authority (PSTA; © 813/530-9911)

St Petersburg was founded in 1876 by John C Williams and Peter A Demens. They built a railroad which was finished in 1888, the railhead being named after Demens' birthplace in Russia. The area had, however, been explored by the Spanish more than 300 years earlier, and Fort De Soto, built in 1513, can still be visited today.

Because of its Gulf-side location, St Petersburg has long been popular with holidaymakers, and in the 1940s the city actively encouraged vacationers to spend their retirement years here. As a result, St Petersburg is now largely a resort city connected by a series of bridges to Tampa and by causeways to the Holiday Isles to the west. There is some industry, and for many decades the city has been known as a seat of learning. The Stetson University College of Law was founded in 1901, two years before St Petersburg was granted city status. The Museum of Fine Arts was opened in 1961.

St Petersburg is, however, better known as the 'Sun Capital of America', largely because of a record 768 consecutive days of sunshine. Between 1910 and 1986 the *St Petersburg Evening Independent* was given away free on days when the sun did not shine; in seventy-six years, the paper was given away free only 295 times, less than four times a year. St Petersburg is very much a resort city, with its palm-lined streets, bustling waterfront and pier, numerous shops and restaurants, and three excellent museums – the Museum of Fine Arts, the Salvador Dali Museum and the Great Explorations children's museum.

Clearwater, nestling along Clearwater Bay, was granted city status in 1912, and is connected to Tampa by the Courtney Campbell Causeway. Odet Philippe, a surgeon in Napoleon's navy, settled in the area in the mid-1830s and planted citrus groves here. Following the establishment of Fort Harrison in 1841, other settlers arrived, led by James Stevens. The first town was known as Clear Water Harbor, although it did not grow significantly until after the arrival of the Orange Belt Railroad in 1888, and it was not until after World War II that there was urban and industrial expansion.

The Garden Memorial Causeway connects Clearwater, as the city became known, to Clearwater Beach, which offers excellent swimming and sandy beaches for sunbathing. A bustling sportfishing fleet is based at the Clearwater Marina, also the home of Sea-Orama, a museum and aquarium which opened in 1954 and which concentrates on the wildlife of the Gulf. There are all sorts of sea trips on offer, from deep-sea fishing, dolphin-spotting and dinner specials to watching the sun set at sea.

Concerts and Broadway shows are staged at the Ruth Eckerd Hall, and you can spend an interesting and educational afternoon at the Clearwater Marine Science Center. A sunset event has now also been introduced by the Chamber of Commerce that is similar to the famous Sunset Celebration staged nightly in Key West's Mallory Square. The Clearwater Sunset at Pier 60 features magicians, musicians, jugglers and other entertainers, plus refreshments and arts and crafts. Pier 60 has undergone a major renovation and now juts out into the Gulf from the main public section of Clearwater Beach, just south of the Double Tree Resort Surfside. In addition to the sunset festival, the pier is a great location for fishing and sightseeing.

The city of Clearwater has also opened the new Harborview Center as a major conference venue. It sits on a bluff in the downtown area and offers spectacular views over Clearwater Bay.

Clearwater has many fine beaches in addition to Clearwater Beach, including Sand Key Park to the south. This is a wonderful wide beach with covered picnic areas, charcoal grills, toilets and lots of parking spaces.

St Petersburg and Clearwater Sights

Boatyard Village (Fairchild Drive, Clearwater) is a re-created 1890s fishing village nestling in its own cove in Tampa Bay. There are also restaurants, shops, galleries and a theatre. Open: daily 10am–6pm. ✆ 813/535-4678

Boyd Hill Nature Park (1101 Country Club Way South, St Petersburg) is a 216 acre (86 hectare) park with nature trails for walking and cycle paths. Open: daily 9am–5pm. ✆813/893-7326

Celebration Station (Highway 19 North, Clearwater) is a family-orientated theme park with rides, boats, mini golf and dining facilities. Open: Sunday to Thursday noon–9pm, Friday noon–midnight and Saturday 10am–midnight. ✆ 813/791-1799

Coliseum Ballroom (Fourth Avenue, St Petersburg) is one of the nation's largest ballrooms and was used as a set in the film *Cocoon*. It opened in 1924 and still features big bands. ✆ 813/892-5202

Florida International Museum (Second Avenue North) features major travelling exhibitions. ✆ 813/822-3693

Florida Military Aviation Museum (next to the St Petersburg-Clearwater International Airport)

houses restored aircraft and aviation artefacts dating from World War II. Open: Tuesday, Thursday and Saturday 10am–4pm, and Sunday 1pm–5pm. ✆ 813/535-9007

Great Explorations (1120 4th Street South, St Petersburg, just inland from the Salvador Dali Museum) is a must, especially if you have children. Open: Monday to Saturday 10am–5pm, and Sunday noon–5pm. ✆ 813/821-8992

Largo Heritage Park and Museum (125th Street North, Largo) is a fascinating collection of restored homes and buildings on an 21 acre (8 hectare) wooded site. The museum concentrates on the early pioneers. Open: Tuesday to Saturday 10am–4pm and Sunday 1pm–4pm. Admission free. ✆ 813/582-2123.

Marine Aquarium and Science Center (Windward Passage, Clearwater) is a research and rehabilitation facility, although there are very interesting live and model displays of local marine life. Open: Monday to Friday 9am–5pm, Saturday 9am–4pm and Sunday 11am–4pm. ✆ 813/447-0980

Moccasin Lake Nature Park (Park Trail Lane, Clearwater) is an environmental and energy education centre set in a 50 acre (20 hectare) park that features lakes, upland forest, wetlands and most of the plant and animal species native to the area. Open: Tuesday to Friday 9am–5pm, and Saturday

Opposite: Clearwater Harbor

and Sunday 10am–6pm. Closed Monday. ✆ 813/462-6024

Museum of Fine Arts (255 Beach Drive NE, St Petersburg) houses a fine collection of American and European works dating from the eighteenth to twentieth centuries, as well as ancient, oriental and Renaissance art and furniture. There is also an exhibition of early photographs and the famed collection of Steuben crystal. There are guided tours of the museum, which nestles in its own peaceful gardens. Open: Monday to Saturday 10am–5pm and Sunday 1pm–5pm. ✆ 813/896-2667

Planetarium (St Petersburg Junior College, Fifth Avenue) has shows between September and May. ✆ 813/341-4320

Ruth Eckerd Hall (McMullen Booth Road, Clearwater) is a performing arts centre presenting music, dance and educational programmes for all ages. Visual arts exhibits are regularly displayed in the spacious galleries. The hall is also the home of the Florida Orchestra and offers performances by the Florida Opera. ✆ 813/791-7400 for further details.

St Petersburg Historical and Flight One Museum (2nd Avenue NE, St Petersburg) features a permanent interactive exhibition chronicling the city's history. The Benoist Pavilion houses a replica of the world's first commercial airliner, which made the first commercial flight from St Petersburg to Tampa on 1 January 1914.

St Petersburg Pier (Second Street) is one of the city's most famous landmarks and is big in every sense of the word, being as long as an airport runway. It has a road running down its entire length with lots of carparking on either side.It reopened in 1988 after a multi-million-dollar renovation, and features shops, a farmer's market, a dining court, an observation deck, a public boat dock and catwalks for fisherman. Open: daily 10am–9pm. Admission is free. ℂ 813/821-6164. At the beach end of the pier is a museum run by the St Petersburg Historical Society. Open: Monday to Saturday 10am–5pm and Sunday 1pm–5pm. ℂ 813/894-1052

Salvador Dali Museum (to the south of the pier on 3rd Street North, St Petersburg) houses the world's most comprehensive collection of Dali's work. Open: Tuesday to Saturday 10am–5pm, and Sunday and Monday noon–5pm. ℂ 813/823-3767

Sawgrass Lake Park (St Petersburg) is a 360 acre (144 hectare) park. There is 1 mile (2km) of elevated boardwalks running through a maple swamp to an observation tower. A self-guided walk booklet is available for the nature trails. ℂ 813/527-3814

Science Center (22 Avenue, St Petersburg) houses permanent exhibits that include a nature trail, a static electricity display, antique microscopes and scientific equipment, and minerals, ores and corals. Open: Monday to Friday 9am–4pm. ℂ 813/384-0027

Sea Screamer (operates from Kingfish Wharf, Treasure Island) claims to be the world's largest speedboat. It offers daily bird- and marine-life trips around nearby islands and out into the Gulf.

Suncoast Botanical Gardens (125th Street North, Largo) covers 60 acres (24 hectares), and although it specializes in local plants it also features species from other parts of the world, particularly cacti. Open: daily. ℂ 813/595-7218

Suncoast Seabird Sanctuary (Gulf Boulevard, Indian Shores) is a world-famous, non-profit-making bird hospital and often has 500 patients under treatment. This is a good place to see the region's birdlife at close hand. Open: daily. ℂ 813/391-6211

Sunken Gardens (4th Street, St Petersburg) is a collection of more than 50,000 tropical plants, many of which bloom year round. Open: daily 9am–5.30pm. ℂ 813/896-3186

Shopping in St Petersburg and Clearwater

The area has shops to suit all tastes and pockets. Most shops and all malls open seven days a week, and all malls have a variety of eating opportunities.

Malls

Bay Area Outlet Mall
Roosevelt Boulevard, Clearwater

Clearwater Mall
Highway 19 and Gulf to Bay Boulevard, Clearwater

Countryside Mall
Highway 19 and State Road 580, Clearwater

Gateway Mall
Nine Street North, St Petersburg

Largo Mall
Ulmerton and Seminole Boulevard, Largo

Pinellas Square Mall
Highway 19 and Park Boulevard, Pinellas Park

Seminole Mall
Seminole and Park Boulevards, Seminole

Sunshine Mall
Missouri Avenue, Clearwater

Tyrone Square Mall
22nd Avenue and Tyrone Boulevard, St Petersburg

Shopping villages:

Boatyard Village
Fairchild Drive, Clearwater Restaurants, boutiques and galleries. Open: Monday to Saturday 10am–6pm and Sunday 10am–5pm.

Hamilin's Landing
2nd Street East, Indian Rocks Beach. Waterfront shopping and dining complex. Open: daily

John's Pass Village and Boardwalk
Gulf Boulevard, Madeira Beach. Quaint shopping district with galleries and boutiques. Open: daily

Beaches and Keys

Indian Rocks Beach consists of seven different communities which make up a very peaceful resort area, ideal for family holidays. Sights include the Suncoast Seabird Sanctuary on Gulf and the 60 acre (24 hectare) Suncoast Botanical Gardens ; alternatively, you can take a paddle-wheel dinner cruise on the Intercoastal Waterway. Hamlin's Landing (Second Street East) is a new waterfront, shopping and dining complex on the Intracoastal Waterway. The original Victorian buildings have been revamped to include luxury flats, speciality shops and entertainment venues. There are also docking facilities. Open: daily.

Madeira Beach is the fishing capital of this stretch of coast, and its scenic harbour is full of commercial and charter fishing boats. There is an old-fashioned boardwalk with charming shops and a host of restaurants, and almost 3 miles (5km) of sandy beaches. John's Pass Village and Boardwalk is a must.

In 1848 George Watson was commissioned to carry out the first official survey of South Florida. The Gulf Beach Islands were considered worthless and so were not included, but Watson met and became friends with Juan Levique and Joe Silva, sea-turtle hunters based in what is now Madeira Beach, and he did a free hand sketch of the area for them. Later that year a hurricane hit and dramatically re-arranged the coastline, and when Juan returned from a hunting trip he noticed a new cut between the Gulf of Mexico and his base in Boca Ciega Bay. This was named after him, later being Americanized to John's Pass. A bridge built over the pass in 1875 was replaced in 1927 and again in 1971, latterly by the Gulf Boulevard which revitalized the area, bringing in shops, restaurants and attractions. Today, John's Pass is one of the area's leading attractions and still remains the headquarters of the local fishing and charter-boat fleets. There are more than a hundred stores, plus a wide range of eateries and a wealth of watersports. The John's Pass Seafood Festival, held each autumn, is one of the largest in Florida, and a Christmas parade of lighted boats is a local tradition.

Treasure Island is an unspoiled beach nearly 4 miles (6km) long, suitable for those who want to get away from it all. The beach is very wide and allows everyone room to spread out, but it also offers plenty of watersports and activities for those who want them, as well as fishing charters and sightseeing cruises.

St Petersburg Beach has almost 7 miles (11km) of splendid beaches. You can visit historic Fort De Soto, built in 1513, enjoy deep-sea fishing, dine and dance aboard the dinner boats, or just enjoy the sun, sea and sand. The Silas Bayside Market on Gulf Boulevard is an unusual shopping village in a tropical setting and features speciality shops and a food court.

Cabbage Key was once an Indian settlement; an old Indian shell mound can still be seen. Author Mary Roberts Rinehart also lived here, and her home is now the Cabbage Key Inn. The small island is of interest because of its wildlife and history, and can be explored via a nature trail.

Fort De Soto Park lies south of St Petersburg Beach on Mullet Key, which juts out into the Gulf, and features a fort built during the Spanish-American War. The park covers 900 unspoiled acres (360 hectares), with 7 miles (11km) of

St Petersburg
and
Clearwater

Key to Map

1. Boatyard Village
2. Boyd Hill Nature Park
3. Florida Military Aviation Museum
4. Great Explorations
5. Largo Heritage Park and Museum
6. Marine Aquarium and Science Center
7. Moccasin Lake Nature Park
8. Museum of Fine Arts
9. Ruth Eckerd Hall
10. Fort De Soto Park
11. St Petersburg Historical and Flight One Museum
12. St Petersburg Pier
13. Salvador Dali Museum
14. Sawgrass Lake Park
15. Science Center
16. Sea Screamer
17. Suncoast Botanical Gardens
18. Suncoast Seabird Sanctuary
19. Sunken Gardens

beaches, two fishing piers, camping and picnic areas, and some of the best migration bird-watching in the state. There are walking trails, rental bikes, snack bars, boat ramps and toilets. Access is via Highway 679a, the toll bridge which leads to the island park. ℂ 813/866-2662.

Egmont Key State Park stands at the mouth of Tampa Bay southwest of Fort De Soto Beach, and is accessible only by private boat or ferry. This 440 acre (176 hectare) island is a wildlife refuge, and is also home to the only manned lighthouse in the USA. Formerly a camp for captured Seminoles during the Third Seminole War, and then a base for the Union Navy during the Civil War, the park is now jointly managed by the Florida Department of Natural Resources, the US Fish & Wildlife Service and the US Coast Guard. Swimming, fishing and boating are all excellent.

St Petersburg and Clearwater Restaurants

Bon Appetit, ($$; International), 150 Marina Plaza, Dunedin
ℂ 813/736-4365

Brunello
($$–$$$; Italian), 3861 Gulf Boulevard,
St Petersburg
ℂ 813/367-1851

Columbia Restaurant
($$; Spanish), 1241 Gulf Boulevard, Clearwater Beach
ℂ 813/596-8400

Crabby Bill's, ($$; Seafood), 412 1st Street,
Indian Rocks Beach
ℂ 813/595-4825

Chateau Madrid,
($$; International),
19519 Gulf Blvd, Indian Shores
ℂ 813/596-9100

El Pass-O, ($$; Mexican),
13331 Gulf Blvd, Madeira Beach
ℂ 813/392-8986

Gathering Restaurant
($–$$; American),
14100 Walsingham Road,
Indian Rocks Beach
ℂ 813/593-1600

Jesse's Landing
($$; seafood), 10400 Park Boulevard, St Petersburg
ℂ 813/393-0896

King Charls Restaurant
($$; International),
Don CeSar Beach Resort,
3400 Gulf Blvd,
St Petersburg Beach
ℂ 813/360-1881

Lenny's
($; American), 21220 Highway 19N
ℂ 813/799-0402

Leverocks of Clearwater Beach
($$; seafood), 551 Gulf
Boulevard, Clearwater Beach
℡ 813/446-5884

Leverocks Seafood House
($$; seafood), 565 150th
Avenue, Madeira Beach
℡ 813/393-0459 Also at 7000
Highway 19N, St Petersburg
℡ 813/526-9188

Luby's Cafeteria
($; American), 7770 66th Street
N, St Petersburg
℡ 813/544-2600

94th Aero Squadron
($$; seafood and steaks),
94 Fairchild Drive, Clearwater
℡ 813/524-4155

Peking Palace
($–$$; Chinese), 1608 Gulf to
Bay Boulevard, Clearwater
℡ 813/461-4414

Silas Dents
($$; seafood and steaks),
5501 Gulf Boulevard, St
Petersburg Beach
℡ 813/360-6961

Steak & Ale,
($$; Steak/Seafood)
445 99th Avenue N,
St Petersburg
℡ 813/578-7302

Thai Nana
($$; Thai), 2856 Alternate
Highway 19N
℡ 813/787-0189

Tio Pepe
($–$$; Spanish), 2930 Gulf to
Bay Boulevard, Clearwater
℡ 813/799-3082

The spectacular Sunshine Skyway Bridge straddles Tampa Bay and makes landfall just north of Bradenton, allowing our journey to continue south down the Gulf Coast. The next chapter covers Tampa and its attractions, as well as all points south.

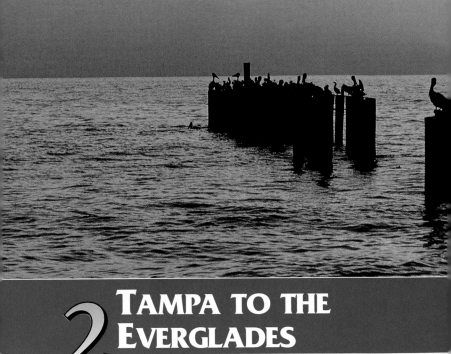

TAMPA TO THE EVERGLADES

2 The sights and cities covered in this section follow Florida's Gulf Coast south from Tampa to the Everglades.

Tampa

The warm waters, golden sands and year-round sunshine of the central Gulf Coast make the Tampa area an ideal holiday location. It is an area steeped in rich history, with many a tale of pirates and buried treasure, and also manages to cater to all tastes. The beaches, sea and attractions make it ideal for families, the wealth of open-air activities have earned it the title 'World Capital of Sport', and at night there is wining, dining, dancing and a host of other entertainments to attract you, whatever your interests.

In the early sixteenth century, the first European explorers visited the Gulf Coast. Juan Ponce de León probably sailed into Tampa

Above: Sunset at Naples

Bay during his exploration along the west coast of Florida in 1521, and in the spring of 1539 Hernando de Soto, Governor of Cuba, sailed into Tampa Bay in search of gold. The Indian fishing settlement there was called *Tanpa*, meaning 'Sticks of Fire', and this somehow got changed to Tampa over the years.

In 1772 the Dutch cartographer Bernard Romans named the area around Tampa Bay Hillsborough in honour of Lord Hillsborough, Secretary of State for the Colonies. Many of the early settlements were attacked by Indians, and it was not until the Seminole Wars of the nineteenth century that an army base was established at Fort Brooke in 1824. Many soldiers who were posted to the area returned after the wars to settle there, so that by 1846 Tampa had acquired town status and the pace of settlement had speeded up. During the Civil War, the Confederates surrendered the fort after being bombarded by Union gunboats.

- Tampa hosts the Florida State Fair every February.

- Tampa is invaded by pirates every February during the month-long Gasparilla Festival.

- Tampa has the seventh-largest port in the USA and the largest in Florida.

- Tampa has the longest continuous sidewalk and the smallest park in the USA.

- Tampa is the home port of the world's only fully rigged pirate ship, the José Gasparilla, which sets sail every year during the Gasparilla Festival.

- Hillsborough County produces ninety per cent of tropical fish found in aquariums in the USA.

The railroad arrived in 1883, the brainchild of Henry Plant. The Southern Florida Railroad, connecting Tampa with markets throughout the USA, attracted new business and industry as well as rich entrepreneurs. A causeway was built over the Gulf and piers constructed for ocean-going vessels. Plant also started a steamship line between Tampa, Key West and Havana. The port expanded rapidly and the railroad helped the area develop as a tourist resort.

In 1885 Vincente Martinez Ybor moved to the area from Key West, and the following year he established the first cigar factory. Cigars are still made in Ybor City (pronounced 'Ee-bor'), now Tampa's Cuban quarter. An old Tampa joke runs along the lines of: 'my mother was a stripper and my father a boxer', referring to different jobs on the cigar-rolling assembly line. At one time almost 12,000 people worked in the 200 cigar factories.

In 1891 Henry Plant opened the 511-room Tampa Bay Hotel, based on a Moorish Temple, and in 1898 Colonel Theodore 'Teddy' Roosevelt and his Rough Riders trained in the extensive grounds before sailing for Cuba during the Spanish-American War. The hotel, the first in Tampa to have electric power, is now used as offices by the University of Tampa and also houses a small museum. It is a National Historic Landmark.

Tampa's waterfront includes a picturesque harbour and elegant walkways, shops and restaurants, as well as the port. New terminals are being built to handle the growing number of boats sailing into the port – particularly cruise ships. You can dine by the water's edge or take a dinner cruise aboard a paddle-wheeler or luxury yacht. The new Garrison Seaport Center incorporates the Florida Aquarium, the $70-million Whydah Pirate Collection and a new cruise ship terminal, plus a 16,000-seat amphitheatre, cinema complex, shops and restaurants.

Downtown Tampa has long been noted for its patronage of the arts, and a brochure listing what is on show is available from the Art in Public Places office or from local museums and galleries. Many of these works of art are displayed in the lobbies of company offices, but members of the public are allowed access during normal business hours. Among the many fine works on show are Geoffrey Naylor's 90ft high (27m) aluminium wall relief sculpture in the lobby of the First Florida Bank, on the corner of Tampa and Madison streets; William Severson's solar-powered hanging sculpture on the corner of Franklin and Zack streets; and Charles Fager's ceramic work in the lobby of Tampa City Center. Tampa's Museum of Science and Industry has been trebled in size and includes a 350-seat Omnimax Theater, where films are projected on an 85ft-high (26m) domed screen – another first for Florida. The Tampa Museum of Art has also been remodelled and expanded.

Tampa has a population of around 280,000, while surrounding Hillsborough County has a total population of 834,000. It offers a wide range of activities and entertainments, and attracts well over 4 million visitors a year. While the area is a rich farming region, especially strawberries and citrus fruits, there are also around thirty-six golf courses, including ones designed by Arnold Palmer and Robert Trent Jones. The Saddlebrook Golf and Tennis Resort, 12 miles (19km) north of Tampa, is set in 480 acres (192 hectares) and is now the world headquarters for the Arnold Palmer Golf Academy, which offers courses of varying durations for all ages and abilities. There are rivers to canoe along, hiking and horse-riding trails, and an abundance of wildlife to spot. There are more than 1,000 public and private tennis courts, and waterfront boulevards for running and cycling. In addition, Hillsborough's one hundred parks offer freshwater fishing, swimming, canoeing, horseback riding and hiking.

While Tampa itself does not have many beaches, it does have a number of resort complexes as well as several major attractions. However, there are public beaches at Ben T Davis Beach on State Road 60W, Picnic Island in South Tampa and EG Simmons Park off Interstate 75S. The nearby Gulf and lakes offer swimming, jet-skiing, windsurfing and parasailing. You can rent motorboats,

Above: The Florida Aquarium, Tampa *Below:* Tampa skyline

Above: St Pete's Pier **Below:** Myombe Reserve, Busch Gardens

paddleboats and pontoons, and, further out, you can try your hand at scuba-diving or deep-sea fishing among the numerous reefs and wrecks.

Getting Around

Tampa lies on Florida's Gulf Coast in Hillsborough County, which covers 1,000sq miles (2,592sq km) of land and includes two interstate highways and an express toll road. Almost every attraction and hotel lies within 5 miles (8km) of either Interstate 275, which runs north to south, or Interstate 4, which runs east to west. Tampa's Crosstown Expressway runs from Gandy Boulevard east to the Brandon area. The speed limit in residential areas and business districts is 30mph (48kph). There is plentiful parking throughout the area, and metered parking is enforced Monday to Friday 8am–5pm.

Tampa International Airport is one of the best in the USA and the largest on the Gulf Coast. The facilities are excellent and it is consistently voted one of the best international airports in the world. Whether you arrive on a domestic or international flight, there is very clear signposting with moving walkways and shuttles to most areas, including the massive new parking complex. All the major car-hire companies have branches at the airport and there are courtesy coaches to most

of the hotels, as well as taxi and limousine services.

The HART (Hillsborough Area Regional Transit) Line provides most of the public transport in the area. There are forty-two bus routes throughout the Tampa area, the main terminus located in Marion Street in downtown Tampa. The PeopleMover monorail provides transportation downtown and to and from Harbour Island. Greyhound buses operate out of Tampa from 610 Polk Street, while Amtrak trains stop at the station at the junction of Nebraska Avenue and Twiggs Street.

Busch Gardens

This is undoubtedly the Gulf Coast's main attraction and should not be missed. A 300 acre (120 hectare) combination of theme parks, rides, non-stop entertainment, a zoo and the world's largest brewery, Busch Gardens has a lot to offer and is constantly being updated to appeal to the thrill-seekers in particular. As there is so much to see and do throughout the day, you should pick up the entertainments programme on arrival so that you can fit in as many shows as possible between rides.

Busch Gardens is based on turn-of-the-century Africa – the 'Dark Continent' – and there are nine themed areas, the latest being

Egypt, with its heart-stopping inverted-corkscrew roller-coaster. The zoo is the fourth largest in the USA. One of the best ways of seeing the hundreds of animals is to take the Skyride Cable-car, which allows you to look down on the wildlife as it roams 'free' on the Serengeti Plain. You can also take the Trans-Veldt Railroad which circles the park. Moats and natural barriers, rather than bars, are used to keep the animals in. Members of the Conservation Information staff can be found throughout the park offering brief presentations and are always willing to answer any questions you may have.

Below is a description of each of the themed areas, touring Busch Gardens in an anticlockwise direction as this is the most convenient.

Morocco is the first of the themed areas and lies immediately inside the main entrance. Belly dancers and snake charmers perform daily in the Sultan's Tent, the Mystic Sheiks Marching Band can be seen and the Moroccan Palace Theater features an ice spectacular, *Hollywood on Ice,* the park's most popular show. Other attractions include the Tangiers Theater and a wide range of shops and gift stores. If you feel hungry, try the Zagora Café or the Boujad Bakery, where delicious pastries are cooked daily. The Ice Cream Parlor specializes in strawberry-topped waffle cones crammed with the ice-cream of your choice.

Myombe Reserve is one of the most popular themed areas in the park, and features gorillas and chimpanzees in a spectacular tropical environment which can be viewed from literally only a couple of feet away. There are also audio-visual presentations and park staff on hand to tell you more about the animals.

Crown Colony is situated on the right-hand side of the park between Morocco and Myombe Reserve, and many people rush past it in their haste to get to the rides. You should head here if you want to take the Skyride, Monorail or Questor, or see the magnificent Anheuser-Busch Clydesdale shire-horses. At the Anheuser-Busch Hospitality Center you can enjoy a beer (if you are old enough) and a pizza or deli sandwich. If you would prefer a more substantial meal, dine in the Crown Colony House Restaurant, with its splendid views over the Serengeti Plain.

Nairobi features Asian elephants, a petting zoo and an animal nursery. The nursery is in Nairobi's Field Station; here you can see very young animals and birds that are either ill or have been rejected by their mothers and have to be reared by human surrogate mums. Visit Curiosity Caverns, where you can watch strange creatures flying, eating and exploring in naturalistic surroundings. The Kenya Kanteen offers snacks, drinks and other light refreshments. The Trans-Veldt Railroad runs from the Nairobi station, touring the Serengeti Plain and stopping at the Congo and Stanleyville stations. The 'Backbones of Life' exhibition explains how creatures evolved on earth.

Serengeti Plain is a 160 acre (64 hectare) paddock where the wildlife, including exotic birds, baboons, buffalo, impala, camels, zebras, giraffes, gazelles, hippos and rhinos, can move around almost as freely as they would on the African plains.

Timbuktu lies just beyond the elephant enclosure and has rides for all ages, including the heart-stopping Scorpion, another of the roller-coaster rides for which Busch Gardens has become famous; this one has a 360-degree loop. Timbuktu also includes the Dolphin Theater, which stages the 'Dolphins of the Deep' show several times daily, and Das Festhaus, offering German-style food and entertainment in a family Oktoberfest atmosphere. There are many children's rides, as well as shops, craft bazaars, and arcade and fair games.

The Congo is home to several of the park's most popular attractions. Rare white Bengal tigers prowl on the aptly named Claw Island, and for the strong-hearted, there are the Kumba and Python roller-coasters, the latter a double-corkscrew ride. There are also the white-water rapids on the Congo River to navigate, so, as you are likely to get wet, make sure any cameras are protected. (Lockers are provided for valuables for anyone waiting to take rides on the Kumba or the Congo River Rapids.) Other attractions include Ubanga-Banga Bumper Cars, Monstrous Mamba and many children's rides and games. Apart from the gift shops, there is the Vivi Storehouse Restaurant and Python Ice Cream. You can catch the train from Congo to return to the exit and the new Egypt attraction, or you can continue your walking tour.

Stanleyville, the next themed area, is named after the famous 'Dr Livingstone, I presume' explorer. If you really like getting wet, then head for the Tanganyika Tidal Wave; after a deceptively peaceful journey through Orchid Canyon, the boat starts to climb and then hurtles down a drop to the water splash. Alternatively, climb aboard a 'dug-out canoe' for a journey over the Stanley Falls. Also find time to take in the variety show at the Stanleyville Theater and the improvized comedy routines at the Zambesi

Opposite: *Montu, the world's largest inverted roller coaster at Busch Gardens*

Theater. The Stanleyville Smoke-house offers chicken, beef and ribs that are slow-smoked for hours, while the Bazaar Café sells barbecued-beef sandwiches. Other exhibits include Orchid Canyon, featuring plants and exotic animals from the tropics. Animals on display elsewhere include orangutans and snakes.

The Bird Gardens form the final themed area, and are full of shaded walks and hidden-away places to delight children. There is Fla-mingo Island, Eagle Canyon, the Koala Display and a host of exotic birds. The Bird Show Theater has hourly shows featuring birds of the world, while the Hospitality House Stage offers musical variety, including jazz and ragtime. Land of the Dragons is a dragon-themed adventure land with a number of interactive attractions, as well as rides and a theatre.

There are lots of games and rides for children, as well as shops and gift stores, while the Hospi-tality House and Gingerbread House offer refreshments. One must also not forget that Busch Gardens is the home of the world's largest brewery. At the Hospitality House (if you are aged twenty-one or over) you can try two complimentary samples of beer while listening to the shows, these alternating between the rocking 1960s and country music. You may be asked for identifica-tion to prove your age.

The brewery visit is also worth making time for. You learn how the beer is made and take in a trip to one of the world's most modern bottling plants. From here make your way back through Morocco and Crown Colony to Egypt, the park's newest attraction.

Egypt covers 7 acres (2.8 hec-tares) and re-creates the sights and sounds of Egypt's culture and eras, from its ancient civilisations to twentieth-century influences. The main attraction is Montu, the tallest and longest inverted roller-coaster in the world, which reaches in excess of 60mph (95kph) during the almost three-minute ride. The ride is unique in that it features the world's largest inverted loop at 104 ft (32m), and a 'Batwing' manoeuvre consisting of two 45-degree-angled vertical loops. It also includes an 60ft (18m) vertical loop which plum-mets below ground-level into an excavation trench, and the 'Immelman', an inverse diving loop named after a German stunt pilot. During parts of the ride (which attains a maximum g-force of 3.85) riders actually achieve weightlessness for a few seconds.

Visit Tut's Tomb, a replica of the six-burial-chamber site of the young pharoah as it was being excavated in the 1920s by archae-ologist Howard Carter, and the Sand Dig area, where children can 'discover' Egyptian antiquities buried in the sands of time.

Open: daily 9.30am–6pm (later in the summer). ✆ 813/987-5082

Other Tampa Sights

Next door to Busch Gardens, and owned by the same company, is **Adventure Island**, an 19 acres (8 hectares) water adventure park with beach area, slides, chutes and wave machines that produce very realistic and endless surf. Open: daily 10am–5pm from spring to fall (late opening during summer). ✆ 813/987-5600

Ben T Davis Municipal Beach is Tampa's only saltwater beach, and runs along the 9 mile (14km) Courtney Campbell Causeway linking Tampa with Clearwater. It is popular with locals and hence can get very crowded.

Bobby's Seminole Indian Village (North Orient Road) is a mini tax haven on Indian land, with its own laws and taxes which allow people to buy duty-free goods. ✆ 813/620-3077

Canoe Escape (9335 East Fowler Avenue, Thonotosassa, Tampa) allows you to paddle your own canoe through Hillsborough County's 16,000 acre (6,400 hectare) Wilderness Park. You can hire canoes for either a couple of hours or all day, and spot alligators, otters, deer, turtles and scores of birds. Open: Monday to Friday 8am–5pm, and Saturday and Sunday 8am–6pm. ✆ 813/986-2067

Children's Museum (North Boulevard) is a hands-on museum tailored to younger visitors, with participatory educational and entertaining activities. Open: Monday to Thursday 9am–4.30pm, Friday 9am–3pm, Saturday 10am–5pm and Sunday 1pm–5pm. ✆ 813/935-8441

The **Florida Aquarium** (Garrison Seaport Center, on the downtown waterfront) opened in 1995. It is one of the largest and most modern aquariums in the USA. Open: daily 9.30am–6pm. ✆ 813/273-4000

Harbor Island is a totally renovated area and now contains hotels, luxury apartments and the Harbor Island Market, a very up-market shopping mall. The PeopleMover monorail transports you to and from the island and to downtown Tampa.

Hillsborough River State Park 12 miles (19km), north of Tampa at Thonotosassa) is a 2,990 acre (1,196 hectare) park. Facilities include camping, picnicking, swimming and boating, with canoes for hire. There are about 8 miles (13km) of nature trails. Fort Foster is located in the park, and you can see what fort life was like in the 1830s.

The *José Gasparilla*, docked on Bayshore Boulevard, is said to be the world's only full-rigged pirate ship.

Lowry Park Zoo (7530 North Boulevard) offers the opportunity to see many of Florida's native species in their natural habitats, including the endangered manatee. In the 12 acre (5 hectare) Florida Wildlife Center there are armadillos, white-tailed deer, black bears, river otters, alligators and Florida panthers, as well as many species of birds. Open: daily 9.30am–5pm. ☎ 813/932-0245

The **Museum of Science and Industry** (4801 East Fowler Avenue, opposite the University of Southern Florida) is Florida's largest museum and specializes in participatory exhibits. It has a planetarium, a butterfly encounter exhibit, and many other hands-on natural phenomena, including one that allows you to feel a shark's tooth. Every hour you can also experience what it feels like to be caught in a hurricane. Open: Sunday to Thursday 9am–5pm, Friday and Saturday 9am–9pm. ☎ 813/987-6300

Simmons Regional Park consists of almost 450 acres (180 hectares) of bayfront and channel land, with a fine, sandy but narrow beach. It is good for swimming, bird-watching, fishing and canoeing, and camping is permitted on the marked waterfront sites.

The **Tampa Bay Hotel** (part of the university campus), with its thirteen silver-topped Moorish minarets (one for each month of the Muslim year), cost a staggering $3 million to build in 1891. The hotel was the brainchild of Henry Plant, who also built the railway, which is why guests arrived in private railcars along a spur from the main track. There are free tours of the hotel at 1.30pm on Tuesdays and Thursdays.

The **Tampa Museum of Art** (601 Doyle Carlton Drive) has a wide range of exhibits, both changing and permanent, from contemporary American and European paintings to ancient works of art from Egypt, Greece and Rome. There is also a programme of hands-on exhibits for children in the Lower Gallery. Open: Tuesday to Saturday 10am–5pm and Sunday 1pm–5pm. Closed Monday. ☎ 813/274-8130

The **Whydah Pirate Complex** focuses on the history of the *Whydah*, the only pirate shipwreck ever discovered. The 175,000sq ft (16,000sq m) museum includes a full-scale replica of the 110ft (35m) *Whydah*, while actors will re-create life aboard the vessel and a movie recounts the salvaging operation. A motion-based simulation ride enables visitors to experience a shipwreck.

Ybor City, the Cuban quarter of Tampa famous for cigar-making, bustles with craftsmen who work from houses and small factories that have changed little over the decades. There are still cobblestoned streets, intricate wrought-iron balconies and Spanish tiles in abundance. The Cu-

Opposite: Tampa Rico Cigar Co, welcomes visitors

bans brought their cigar-making skills with them, and soon Ybor City became home to many other immigrant groups, including Germans, Jews and Italians. The history of the city, now part of Tampa, is told in the Ybor City State Museum, which makes a useful first port of call as you can pick up a map and self-guided walking tour of the area here. The museum (corner of 9th Avenue and 19th Street) is dedicated to the city's founder, Don Vicente Martinez Ybor. His settlement attracted thousands of immigrants and their special skills, so that Ybor City quickly established itself as the cigar capital of the world. The first cigar factory opened in 1886, Ybor City remained a flourishing community until the 1930s. The rich history of the city is preserved at the museum, once a bakery (open: Tuesday to Saturday 9am–noon and 1pm–5pm). You can also visit La Casita, a restored cigar-worker's home (open: Tuesday to Saturday 10am–noon and 1pm–3pm).

The first cigar factory was located in Ybor Square (8th Avenue and 13th Street), now a shopping mall specializing in antiques and memorabilia. Many of the restaurants reflect the ethnic traditions of the early settlers. The Don Quixote restaurant, for example, specializes in authentic Cuban cuisine; also try the fresh-baked Cuban bread at La Segunda Central Bakery on 15th Avenue, which will give you a conducted tour of the premises if you ask in good time. There are organized tours around the mechanized cigar factory of Villazon & Co on Armenia Avenue, where the traditional methods of hand-rolling are still demonstrated. Ybor City now boasts its first micro-brewery, housed in a hundred-year-old cigar factory at 2205 N 20th Street. It can produce up to 60,000 barrels a year; tours are available Tuesday to Saturday 11am–6pm.

Tampa Tours

The following are day tours suggested by the Visitor Information Center.

Tour 1: the heart and soul of Tampa

Day 1: Tampa's heart is Ybor City, its colourful Cuban quarter, where you can still smell the flavour of this turn-of-the-century boomtown. Taste the freshly baked Cuban bread, see cigars being rolled by hand, and take in one of the free guided walking tours through the historic neighbourhood. Lunch at one of the many restaurants and then browse through the shops and galleries, before returning to your hotel for dinner and a pleasant evening.

Day 2: Visit the Henry Plant Museum in the minaret-capped Tampa Bay Hotel to learn more about the man who did most to create this thriving city, then cross the Hillsborough River to visit the Tampa Museum of Art. Enjoy lunch at one of the many open-air restaurants or cafés in Old Hyde Park Village, and then spend an afternoon window shopping or buying from the many stores and boutiques. A pleasant way to watch the sun go down is to make your way to the waterfront at Harbor Island, where you can enjoy drinks on the terrace and watch the boats on the bay. If you really want to splash out, dress up for a night at Bern's, renowned for its menu and wine list, reputed to be the longest in the world. Alternatively, visit the theatre or see one of the many productions staged by the Performing Arts Center. There is guaranteed to be something on show to suit all tastes.

Day 3: Spend the day at Busch Gardens, remembering to plan carefully so that you can fit in all the sights and rides between the various shows and presentations.

Tour 2: the Tampa adventure

Day 1: Visit the Museum of Science and Industry, which has over 200 hands-on exhibits to fascinate children and adults alike, and take in the planetarium and the new butterfly experience. Next, spend some time at the Lowry Park Zoo, one of the best city zoos in North America; be sure to see the Florida exhibit

featuring local animals in their natural habitats – you can even stroke a manatee. Take a swim and then enjoy a leisurely dinner at one of the scores of restaurants in the city before taking in some nightlife.

Day 2: Visit Busch Gardens and spend the day enjoying the rides and seeing the animals. Spend a little time relaxing back at your hotel before heading for Ybor City, and a night of dancing, dining and music.

Day 3: Start the day with a trip to Ybor City. Visit the Ybor City State Museum and take in the shops and galleries before enjoying lunch at one of the many ethnic restaurants. Work off your lunch by spending the afternoon paddling down the Hillsborough River in a canoe, keeping an eye out for alligators and turtles.

Tour 3: for water-lovers

Day 1: Take in Ybor City, close to Tampa docks, and then visit the shops before lunching at one of the many ethnic restaurants. In the afternoon, visit the Henry Plant Museum and then make your way down to the waterfront at Harbor Island for a quiet drink on one of the terraces as the sun sets over the bay. Continuing in the nautical theme, enjoy an evening dinner cruise after having freshened up at your hotel.

Day 2: Take a charter from Tampa's Rocky Point recreation

area or one of the other embarkation points. After lunch at sea or in one of the waterfront restaurants, try water-skiing or jet-skiing, or just laze by the water before enjoying dinner and the rest of the evening.

Day 3: Enjoy a day out at Adventure Island, with its exciting rides, surf and sun.

Tour 4: getting around.

Day 1: Visit Busch Gardens and then have dinner at one of the waterfront restaurants.

Day 2: Drive to St Petersburg and take in the Salvador Dali Museum, which houses the world's most comprehensive collection of the artist's work. Visit the famous St Petersburg hands-on museum and then drive on to Tarpon Springs with its sponge-fishing boats, staying for dinner at one of the delightful waterfront restaurants.

Day 3: Have a game of top-class golf, laze on the beach or shop for all those gifts you have to take back. After lunch drive down to Sarasota (forty minutes) and visit the Ringling Circus Museum, before returning for dinner at one of Tampa's many and varied ethnic restaurants.

Shopping in Tampa

Big Top Flea Market
9250 E Fowler Avenue.
Open: daily, 8am–5pm. Has 600 booths of bargain shopping, from Western boots to fresh produce.

Eastlake Square Mall
5701 E Hillsborough Avenue. Open: Monday to Saturday 10am–9pm and Sunday noon–5.30pm. Wide variety of reasonably priced shops, stores and restaurants.

Florida Flea and Farmer's Market, 9309 N Florida Avenue. Open: Friday, Saturday and Sunday 9am–5pm. More than 800 stalls selling a huge variety of goods at bargain prices, as well as collectibles and antiques.

Gulf Coast Factory Shops
5461 Factory Shops Boulevard, Ellenton. Open: Monday to Saturday 10am–9pm and Sunday noon–6pm. Famous-name manufacturer's outlets offering big savings.

Old Hyde Park Village
Swann and Dakota near Bayshore. Open: Monday to Wednesday 10am–6pm, Thursday and Friday 10am–9pm, Saturday 10am–6pm and Sunday noon–5pm. Speciality shops and restaurants in an outdoor setting.

The Shops on Harbour Island
601 South Harbour Island

Boulevard. Open: Monday to Saturday 10am–9pm and Sunday noon–5pm. Shops, galleries, restaurants, a food court and year-round events.

Tampa Bay Center
3302 Dr Martin Luther King Jr Boulevard. Open: Monday to Saturday 10am–9pm and Sunday noon–6pm. A huge shopping complex featuring more than 160 stores.

University Mall
2200 E Fowler Avenue. Open: Monday to Saturday 10am–9pm and Sunday noon–6pm. Fashion is the speciality in 130-plus shops.

West Shore Plaza
253 Westshore Boulevard. Open: Monday to Saturday 10am–9pm and Sunday noon–5.30pm. Tampa Bay's premiere mall, with almost a hundred fine speciality stores.

Ybor Square
1901 N 13th Street. Open: daily 10am–9pm. Shops, ethnic restaurants and the nostalgia market.

Tampa Information

Visitor Information Center, Corner of Ashley and Madison Streets (Exit 25 off Interstate 275).

✆ 813/223-1111. There are also Visitor Centers located inside Ybor Square, Harbour Island and the Tampa Convention Center.

Florida Bicycle Association ✆ 1-800-FOR BIKE for information on where to cycle, clubs and organized rides.

Tampa Restaurants

Alessi Café Beignet
($; deli and pizzas), 8th Avenue and 18th Street
✆ 813/871-2190

Armani's
($$$; international), Hyatt Regency Westshore
✆ 813/281-9165

Branch Ranch Dining Room
($; family restaurant), Exit 10 off Interstate 4, Plant City
✆ 813/752-1957

Café Creole
($$; Cajun), 1330 East 9th Street
✆ 813/247-6283

Carmine's Restaurant
($; Spanish and international), 1802 Seventh Avenue
✆ 813/248-3834

CK's Revolving Restaurant
($$; Continental), Tampa Airport Marriott
✆ 813/879-5151

Columbia Restaurant
($$; Cuban and Spanish), 2117
East 7th Avenue
✆ 813/248-4961
Renowned tourist haunt since
1905

Crawdaddy's
($$; American, seafood and
steaks), 2500 Rocky Point Drive
✆ 813/281-0407

Damons
($$; family restaurant),
The Place for Ribs, Radisson
Bay Harbor Inn
✆ 813/281-0566

Deli Restaurant
($; deli and seafood), Holiday
Inn Ashley
✆ 813/223-1351

Frankie's Patio Bar and Grill
($; American and Continental),
1920 East 7th Avenue
✆ 813/248-3337

Hemingway's
($$; seafood), Tampa Hilton
✆ 813/877-6688

Ho Ho Chinois
($; Chinese and seafood), 720
South Howard Avenue
✆ 813/254-9557

Hooters, ($$; American),
4215 Hillsborough Ave
✆ 813/885-3916

Lauro Ristorante Italiano
($$; Italian),
3915 Henderson Boulevard
✆ 813/281-2100

Mise en Place
($$; American bistro), 442 West
Kennedy Boulevard
✆ 813/254-5373

Palm Grill
($; American, seafood & steaks)
Best Western Resort
✆ 813/933-4011

Pastabilities
($; Italian), Hyatt Regency
Tampa
✆ 813/ 225-1234

Rio Bravo Cantina
($$; Mexican), 1102 North Dale
Mabry
✆ 813/877-4211

1776 Restaurant
($; American), Ramada Inn,
Plant City
✆ 813/752-3141

Selèna's, ($-$$; American),
1623 Snow Avenue
✆ 813/251-2116

Skipper's Smokehouse
($; American, Cajun, Caribbean
and seafod), 910 Skipper Road
✆ 813/971-0666

Tropics Steak and Seafood
($$), Days Inn by Bahir Beach
✆ 813/645-8119

Yogurt Etcetera
($; specialities), 115 East
Whiting Street.

Manatee County

The area south of Tampa forms
Manatee County, with lots of little
beaches to discover if you have the
time. Worth visiting is the **Gamble
Plantation State Historic Site**, off
Highway 301, once the home of
Major Robert Gamble. He settled
in the area in 1844 after moving
from Tallahassee, and established
a 3,500 acre (1,400 hectare) sugar
plantation, largely created by
slaves borrowed from his father.
The massive house was built over
six years from oyster shells, sand
and molasses – a mixture known as
tabby. Although there was a well in
the grounds, Gamble didn't like
the sulphur-tainted water, so he
had a huge cistern built next to his
house to collect rainwater as it ran
off the roof of the mansion. Min-
nows were kept in the cistern to eat
algae and mosquito larvae. The
walls are 2ft (60cm) thick to keep
the heat out and the windows are
placed strategically to catch any
breeze. Judah P Benjamin, the
Confederate Secretary of State, hid
in the house for three days in
1865, before escaping to Britain
after the Civil War. Gamble went

bust in 1856 and the house was
then occupied by Capt Archibald
McNeill, a gun runner. He was
Benjamin's host and was able to
smuggle him out of the country.
When in England, he continued his
legal career and became legal
counsel to Queen Victoria.

The mansion is the oldest
building in Manatee County, and
is the only antebellum plantation
great house on the Florida penin-
sula. It was saved from demolition
by the United Daughters of the
Confederacy because of its his-
torical significance, and was then
donated to the state. The mansion
and grounds are enclosed by a
white picket fence and are in an
immaculate state. Credit must
duly go to the restorers, especially
when you consider that the house
was used as a fertilizer store in
the 1920s and was a ruin when
the United Daughters of the
Confederacy purchased it in
1925. A school now stands on the
site of the old slave quarters.
There are tours of the house,
which is full of period antiques.
Open: daily 9am–5pm (tours
every hour). ✆ 941/723-4536.

Along this stretch of the coast
there are small beach-hugging
communities such as **Apollo Beach**
and **Sun City**, while sprawling
Bradenton is the largest popula-
tion centre, with many historical
sites, museums, recreational sports
and special annual events.

The first settlers in the area

were the Timucan Indians, who are known to have lived here as early as AD 1000. They were farmers and fishermen, as well as being fierce warriors. Ponce de León is said to have landed on Florida's west coast in 1521, but was driven off by the Indians. In 1539, Hernando De Soto landed at Shaw's Point in Bradenton and, with his powerful force of troops, quelled and enslaved the Indians. He then set off on his quest to find the fabled city of El Dorado, and the area remained free of habitation until 1842, when Josiah Gates became the county's first permanent settler. Manatee County was established in 1856 and originally covered 5,500sq miles (14,308sq km) before it was split into the counties of Manatee, Harden, Highlands, Okeechobee, Sarasota, DeSoto, Charlotte and Glades.

Today, Bradenton boasts fine shopping and good restaurants, and has 43km (27 miles) of white powder-sand beaches, including the Gulf islands of Anna Maria and Longboat Key. The beaches are backed by rolling dunes covered with sea oats and fringed with tall Australian pines which provide shade. The main beaches are Anna Maria Beach, Bayfront Park, Beer Can Island, Coquina Beach, Cortez Beach, Holmes Beach, Manatee County Beach, North Longboat Key Beach and Palma Sola Causeway. The area is also noted for its shelling – you can find sand dollars and a wide variety of other types here, especially on Anna Maria Island and Longboat Key.

For those who prefer a little more action, there is a wide range of watersports, boat docks, marinas, fishing piers, boat excursions, boat rentals and fishing-boat charters along the Gulf of Mexico and Intracoastal Waterway and up the Manatee River. In addition, there is swimming, water-skiing, sailing, canoeing, windsurfing, scuba-diving and pleasure boating. Bradenton is also the home of the world-renowned Nick Bollettieri Tennis Academy and has more then twenty golf courses lying within a short distance, some of them offering quite a challenge. The Legacy, a new eighteen-hole golf course designed by Arnold Palmer, opened in the Lakewood Ranch development at the end of 1996. It features an island hole surrounded by the waters of a 160 acre (64 hectare) lake. The course, off Exit 41 of Interstate 75, is open to visiting players. ℭ 941/907-7920. The Desoto Memorial Dragstrip on State Road 64 has drag racing ℭ 941/ 748-1320, and there is stock-car racing at the DeSoto Speedway on Saturday nights. ℭ 941/748-3171

The area is also a mecca for wildlife. In the warm waters you can spot manatees, and many of the nearby state parks feature recreation areas where you can hire canoes or hike along one of the

Above: *Manatees at Homosassa Springs State Wildlife Park*
Below: *Sunset on Anna Maria Island, Bradenton*

many well-marked nature trails. You may also see alligators, turtles, wild boar and a huge array of native birds.

There is a wide range of accommodation in and around Bradenton and on the Gulf islands, and there is camping at the Linger Lodge, a rustic fishing and RV resort just east of Exit 41 of Interstate 75. The Lodge has great fishing for black bass, blue gill, croppies and catfish, while its museum-like restaurant, The Pavilion, is worth a visit to see the hundreds of stuffed animals, birds and fish that line its walls.

Bradenton now also boasts the world's longest fishing pier on what used to be the south section of the original Sunshine Skyway bridge. The bridge was destroyed when a phosphate tanker rammed into one of the supports during a storm in May 1980. The central section of the southbound span collapsed into the mouth of Tampa Bay, taking the lives of thirty-five people who happened to be driving on that section of the bridge at the time. The bridge has long since been rebuilt, and now spans 3,300ft (1,006m) from shore to shore. The orginal south section is 1.5 miles (2km) long, is open twenty-four hours a day and is lit at night. It costs $3 to take your car along the bridge and $2 per person to fish. You can reach the pier from Exit 1a or 1b off Interstate 275. © 813/865-0668

Just to the north of Bradenton is **Palmetto**, which lies to the north of the 1.6km-wide (mile-wide) Manatee River and is the home of the county's agricultural industry, tomatoes being the main crop. It is also the home of the **Manatee Convention Center**, which attracts top-name entertainers and trade shows.

Bradenton Sights

Cortez is an historic fishing village which has changed little over the years. You can still watch the boats coming in and buy the catches on the dock.

The **De Soto National Memorial** (75th Street) is staffed by rangers who re-enact the lifestyle of De Soto's troops. Open: daily 6am–5.30pm. © 941/792-0458

Manatee Village Historic Park is an historic area with old houses, a church, an 1860 court-house, a country store and a one-room schoolhouse. Open: weekdays 9am–4pm and Sunday 1pm–4pm. Admission is free. © 941/749-7165

Regatta Point Marina offers deep-sea fishing charters and pontoon 'safari' cruises up the Manatee River.

Schomburg Farms (2504 24th Avenue E) offers horse-riding along wooded trails, hay-rides, dairy tours, a barnyard zoo, picnic areas and a campfire. Open: daily. © 941/729-2884

The **South Florida Museum** (10th Street) houses Indian artefacts and the Bishop Planetarium with its spectacular laser shows. The museum traces the history of the area from prehistoric times to the present day. It also houses the Parker Manatee Aquarium. The complex includes the Spanish Courtyard, with replicas of a sixteenth-century Spanish church and the home of Hernando De Soto. Open: daily 10am–5pm between Christmas and Easter, and Tuesday to Saturday 10am–5pm and Sunday 1pm–5pm during the rest of the year. © 941/746-4131

Beyond the Town

Take Highway 64 or 684 west to **Anna Maria Island**, with its fine beaches. This is the main beach area for Bradenton and has excellent seafood restaurants. The beaches include: Anna Maria Beach at the northern end of the island, with long stretches of beaches, dunes, sea oats and Australian pines between the Gulf and the Intercoastal Waterway; and Holmes Beach, noted for its free-roaming peacocks. Holmes Beach is the largest of the island's three municipalities and is also home to the Manatee County Public Beach. The community of Bradenton Beach, at the southern tip of the island, has a number of charming shops, restaurants and accommodation. The Anna Maria Island

Historical Museum (402 Pine Avenue, next door to the Old Anna Maria Jail) is housed in a former 1920s ice house and traces the history of the island. Open: Tuesday to Thursday and Saturday 10am–4pm from September to May, and on the same days 11am–2pm from June to August. Admission is free. © 941/778-0492

The Coquina Baywalk at **Leffis Key** is part of a conservation programme aimed at restoring areas of mangrove-forested shoreline along Sarasota Bay, as these provide a major habitat for both birds and marine life. There are paths and boardwalks through the mangroves and around the tidal lagoons. The park is reached by taking Highway 789 (Gulf of Mexico Drive) south on Anna Maria Island; the entrance is on the left-hand side of the road.

A chain of keys connects Bradenton and Sarasota to the south. The next island is **Longboat Key**, where De Soto's scout is said to have come ashore in a longboat. The key has some exclusive shops and many luxury homes, which you can see as you motor along the Gulf of Mexico Drive. The island straddles Manatee County and Sarasota County, and has 12 miles (19km) of white-sand beaches.

Lake Manatee State Recreation Area, 15 miles (24km) east of Bradenton on State Road 64, is a 556 acre (222 hectare) recreation area stretching 3 miles (5km)

along the southern shores of the lake. It is an excellent place for camping, picnicking, swimming, fishing and boating. **Little Manatee River State Recreation Area,** 4 miles (6km) south of Sun City on Lightfoot Road, Wimauma (off Highway 301), is a 1,638 acre (655 hectare) park which offers camping, canoeing, hiking, picnicking, fishing and bird-watching.

Between Bradenton and Sarasota is **Sarasota/Bradenton International Airport,** which is served by most of the major US airlines and receives services from Canada. The airport also has on-site car-hire facilities. ✆ 941/ 359-277

Bradenton Restaurants

Antonio's
($-$$; Pizza/Italian),
4658 Stote Rd, 64E
✆ 941/747-7356

Beach Bistro
($-$$; American),
Holmes Beach
✆ 941/778-2308

Bob Evans,
($-$$; American),
4115 14th Street West
✆ 941/746-7747

Casa Mia
($$; International),

3911 Highway 301
✆ 941/722-1205

Crown and Thistle British Pub and Restaurant
($$; pub grub), 2519 Gulf Drive North, Bradenton Beach
✆ 941/778-5173

Duffy's Tavern
($; American and fast food),
3901 Gulf Drive, Holmes Beach
✆ 941/778-2501

El Sol
($$; Mexican),
7870 North Tamicimi Trail,
Sarasota
✆ 941/359-3000

La Casa Reinaldo
($$; Italian), 5506 14 Street W,
Bradenton
✆ 941/727-0550

Maggie's Buffet
($-$$; American), 4348 14th
Street W
✆ 941/755-3767

Rotten Ralph's
($$; Steak and seafood),
902 South Bay Blvd,
Anna Maria Island
✆ 941/778-3953

Shells
($$; seafood), Holmes Beach,
East Bay Drive
✆ 941/778-5997

Sarasota County

Sarasota is a county of contrasts. While there is a cosmopolitan, sprawling city of 100,000 on the mainland, there are also laid-back keys with thatch-roofed bars, open-air eateries and glorious beaches, where time seems to have little importance at all. The region boasts 361 days of sunshine a year and consists of the city of Sarasota, part of Longboat Key, Lido Key, St Armands Key, Siesta Key, Venice, Englewood and North Port.

Sarasota was first settled by prehistoric Indians. The Spanish explorer Hernando de Soto is said to have named the area after his daughter Sara, although this stretch of coastline did not see significant permanent settlement for more than 300 years. One of the earliest American settlers was William H Whittaker, who arrived in 1843. By 1885 Sarasota was being described by the Florida Mortgage and Investment Company as a 'modern' town, and this encouraged a group of Scots to try their luck here. When they arrived, however, they found only a country store and a dirt road. Some of the Scots left, but the remainder stayed and started to clear the palmetto bushes and scrub pine to make way for a new town. One of these settlers was John Hamilton Gillespie, who by 1886 had organized the construc-

tion of several more roads, houses and the first hotel, called the De Soto. Gillespie was also responsible for introducing the Scottish game of golf to Florida, and built the state's first course in the 1880s near what is now the Sarasota County Courthouse. The course originally had only two holes and the game was considered a great novelty at the time.

In 1910, Chicago socialite and widow Bertha Palmer arrived, buying an area of land in what is now Osprey to build a winter home. Her patronage was enough for many other wealthy families to follow suit, and by the 1920s there was a real-estate boom throughout the area. This was further boosted by the arrival of entrepreneurs John and Charles Ringling, who chose Sarasota as the winter headquarters for their world-famous Ringling Brothers Barnum and Bailey Circus. John's home, Ca' d'Zan, is one of the most magnificent on the coast.

Today, the area continues to attract the rich and famous, who build fabulous homes overlooking the Gulf. However, it is also a fast-growing residential community and a mecca for artists, writers and musicians.

The area has 150 miles (241km) of waterfront, six barrier islands, 35 miles (56km) of beaches and claims the whitest sand in all of Florida. There are public beaches at Casperson

Beach, Crescent Beach, Lido Beach, Manasota Key, Nokomis Beach, North Jetty Beach, North Lido Beach, South Lido Beach, Turtle Beach and Venice Beach. They are all ideal for sunbathing, swimming, shelling, sailing, snorkelling and fishing, and in the Venice area you can even find fossilized sharks' teeth along the shore – thus its name of 'Shark Tooth Capital of the World'.

The Gulf islands, especially **Lido Key** and **St Armands Key**, are now world-class tourist destinations, with beautiful beaches, top resorts and hotels, superb shops, galleries and restaurants, and acres of recreation area along the bay. Another great attraction of the islands is their lush, tropical vegetation and the fact that many of the houses have secret, tucked-away courtyards and patios. North Lido Beach lies some distance away from most of the traffic and crowds; you can park at the north end of the public beach. At the public beach at Mid-Key there is also a swimming-pool, playground and shops, and lifeguards are on duty year round. At the southern end of Lido Key, there are 100 acres (40 hectares) of Australian pines, with picnic tables, barbecue grills, a volleyball court and a playground provided, plus wooden walkways, nature trails and canoeing at South Lido Park.

Longboat Key is known as the 'Rolls-Royce of Islands'. It stetches more than 10 miles (16km) north from St Armands Key and, apart from its wonderful beaches and luxury homes, it has many award-winning restaurants. The island is quiet and secluded, offering visitors privacy among manicured, tropical beauty, yet also has first-rate golf courses and refined amenities. It is a great place to explore by bike, or you can rollerboard along a 10 mile (16km) cycle path. There is also excellent fishing from the beach, piers and jetties, and the marinas offer rental and charter boats. Just south of Longboat Key is City Island, home of the Mote Marine Aquarium.

Siesta Key is connected to the mainland by two bridges and has the widest beaches in the county. Since 1987, the sugar-fine sand has been rated the 'whitest, finest sand in the world' in an independent assessment which compared it with other locations such as the Bahamas and Grand Cayman. There are two main shopping districts: Siesta Key Village, with more than a hundred shops; and Siesta South, close to Stickney Point Bridge, with more than fifty outlets. A wide range of activities are available at the public beach in the middle of the island, including volleyball, tennis, a playground and shaded picnic tables. There is ample parking, lifeguards are on duty year round, and there are great opportunities for walking, shelling and beachcombing. At the southern end of the island you can snorkel off Crescent Beach. Turtle Beach, off Midnight Pass Road, is a great spot for a picnic or barbecue, and there are walkways across the dunes to the Gulfside beach. Palmer Pointe South is the southernmost point of the island and has wide, undisturbed beaches. Fishing on Siesta Key is also good, especially at Point of Rocks, south of Crescent Beach, and at Big Pass at the northern end.

Sarasota County has more than 12,000 hotel, motel and guest-house rooms and a wide range of restaurants, from fast food on the beach to fine dining. In addition, it has thirty-eight golf courses, tennis courts, boating and fishing facilites, and plenty of profes-sional spectator sports. The Cincinnati Reds hold their spring baseball training in Sarasota County, and there is greyhound racing from January to April at the Sarasota Kennel Club.

The area boasts more cultural attractions than many cities with much larger populations, and has many visual and performing arts opportunities. Most of the its cul-tural venues are housed within the Sarasota City limits(including the Ringling Museum of Art), while the downtown Cultural District is home to the Sarasota Opera House, and numerous theatres, nightclubs, art galleries and restaurants.

Historic Palm Avenue is packed with fine art, antiques, jewellery and fashion outlets, and has always been one of the main shop-ping centres. Sarasota Quay, at the junction of Highway 41 and Fruitville Road, has a number of speciality shops, eateries and nightclubs along its waterfront, while the redesigned and land-scaped City Marina near by offers charter boats and dinner cruises. There is a wide range of shopping elsewhere in the area, from ex-pensive designer names in St Armands Circle to budget prices at the Sarasota Outlet Center.

Sarasota Sights

The **Asolo Theatre and Asolo Center for the Performing Arts** has its own regional repertory company that produces a nine-month season of contemporary and classical works. The theatre is an elegant reconstruction of a turn-of-the-century European theatre.

Bellm's Cars and Music of Yesteryear (5500 North Tamiami Trail, Sarasota) has scores of re-stored and antique cars. The Great Music Hall displays antique music-boxes from the 1890s. ✆ 941/355-6228

Gulf Coast World of Science is great for children, with hands-on exhibits and displays. You can dig for fossils, touch live snakes or carry out your own experiments. ✆ 941/359-9975

Historic Spanish Point (Little Sarasota Bay, Osprey) includes a late-Victorian pioneer home, a Native American burial mound, a nineteenth-century chapel and cemetery, and parts of a landscaped garden from a nineteenth-century estate. ℡ 941/966-5214

Marie Selby Botanical Gardens (on the bay off Highway 41). There are fifteen distinct garden areas covering 11 acres (4.4 hectares), including the famous World Orchid Center with its collection of more than 6,000 orchids. More than 20,000 plants are on display in the open air or under glass. Open: daily 10am–5pm. ℡ 941/366-5731

Mote Marine Aquarium and Laboratory (1600 Ken Thompson Parkway, Sarasota) features a 300,000 gallon (1.4 million litre) outdoor shark tank, a 30ft (10m) touch tank, and river, bay and estuary displays. There is also a marine mammal visitor centre and a marine mammal hospital. Open: daily 10am–5pm. ℡ 941/388-4441

Myakka State Park and Wilderness Preserve (off State Road 72, about 9 miles (14km), east of Sarasota) is Florida's largest park, covering 35,000 acres (14,000 hectares) of wetlands, marsh and woodlands along the Myakka River and Upper Myakka Lake. It has a wealth of wildlife and plants, and is home to more than 200 species of birds. There are lots of nature trails, guided boat and tram rides, a small natural history museum, and boats and bikes for rent. Open: daily 8am–sunset. ℡ 941/365-0100. Tram tours are offered by **Myakka Wildlife Tours** ℡ 941/365-0100.

Pelican Man's Bird Sanctuary (opposite the Mote Aquarium) was established as a sanctuary for injured and recovering birds, while allowing visitors an opportunity to see some of Florida's native wildlife in its natural habitat. ℡ 941/388-4444

Ringling Museum of Art (Bay Shore Road, Sarasota) is also the State Art Museum of Florida and houses one of the country's premier collections of Baroque art. The 66 acre (26 hectare) landscaped estate also contains Ca' d'Zan (meaning 'House of John' in the Venetian dialect), the Venetian Renaissance mansion built by John and Mable Ringling in the mid-1920s. The columns surrounding the inner courtyard are thought to date from the eleventh century. The baroque collection is the most important of the museum's treasures. The Circus Museum can also be visited, with eighteenth-century prints, old costumes and the Barlow Animated Miniature Circus, a scale model of the Ringling Brothers and Barnum and Bailey Circus of the 1930s. There are three gift shops and a café. Open: daily. ℡ 941/359-5700.

Opposite: Sarasota Beach

Sarasota Cultural Attractions and Organisations

- ✪ Sarasota County Arts Council
  ✆ 941/365-5118

- ✪ Sarasota Ballet of Florida
  ✆ 941/359-0771

- ✪ Sarasota Film Society
  ✆ 941/364-8662

- ✪ Project Black Cinema
  ✆ 941/953-6424

- ✪ Florida West Coast Symphony
  ✆ 941/953-4252

- ✪ Sarasota Opera Association
  ✆ 941/366-8450.

- ✪ Asolo Center for the
  Performing Arts
  ✆ 941/351-9010

- ✪ Florida Studio Theatre
  ✆ 941/366-9017

St Amands Circle (St Amands Key) has 120 speciality shops, boutiques and restaurants. You can take a leisurely horse-drawn carriage ride from nearby Lido Beach at sunset around the Circle and one if its highlights, the Circus Ring of Fame, which honours many of the world's most famous circus performers.

The Van Wezel Performing Arts Hall was designed by the Frank Lloyd Wright Foundation and stands in Sarasota Bay. It offers performances by the Florida West Coast Symphony and Florida Symphonic Band, as well as hosting touring Broadway shows and well-known entertainers. The Sarasota Arts Council operates a twenty-four-hour Arts Line (✆ 941/953-4636 ext 6000) for information about what is on, where and when.

South of the City

The Oscar Scherer State Park lies 2 miles (3km) south of the small community of Osprey on Highway 41, and the area around the northern end of Lake Osprey is one of the best places in the state to view scrub jays. You can also spot gopher tortoises and nesting bald eagles. For even better birdwatching and the chance to see the real Florida, rent a canoe and paddle down tidal South Creek past the marshes and mangroves. ✆ 941/483-5956.

Casey Key lies just to the north of Venice, and is a charming beach area with sloping dunes. The Nokomis Beach, at the southern end of the island, covers 20 acres (8 hectares) and has a boat ramp, volleyball court and picnic areas; lifeguards are on duty here all year. The 18 acre (7 hectare) North Jetty Beach, also towards the south of the island, has good surfing, picnic areas and a playground, as well as jetties which afford great fishing spots.

Venice, also in Sarasota County, is a lovely island city on the Gulf. Luxury homes line the canals and natural waterways, these accounting for the city's name and explaining the fine Italian architecture and landscaped boulevards that date back to the original city plans of 1925. The area offers a wealth of water-sports and boating, more than twelve golf courses, floodlit tennis courts and fishing from the many jetties. The beaches are rarely crowded and offer great shelling and fossilized sharks'-teeth finds. Inland, there is fine shopping and dining, as well as a community theatre, a dinner theatre, an art league, opera and theatre guilds, a symphony orchestra and two libraries. Just to the south are pristine **Brohard Beach** and **Caspersen Beach**, with nature trails that wind inland through typical Floridian tropical vegetation.

Englewood Bay and **Lemon Bay** are situated in the southern corner of Sarasota County, and although a little off the beaten track they are well worth visting for their beautiful, uncrowded beaches. Manasota Beach is patrolled year round by lifeguards, and the 14 acre (5.6 hectare) area has toilets, picnic sites and barbecue pits. There are even docks where you can tie up if you arrive by boat. Just east of Englewood is the Texas Rangers complex, where from mid-February to late March this major league team carries out its spring training. The area also offers several golf courses, tennis courts and two recreation centres.

North Port, just inland, is a new and growing community. It has a rich wildlife of deer, armadillos, opossums, turtles, raccoons, bobcats, otters, and gators, with fishing and boating as the main outdoor activities. Freshwater canals run into the Myakka River, itself flowing into the Gulf at Charlotte Harbor. Myakka Creek offers good canoeing, and the area is home to the Warm Mineral Springs, where the heavily mineralized water maintains a constant 87°F (30°C).

Following Page: John Ringling Mansion, Sarasota

Sarasota County Restaurants

Bijou Café
($$–$$$; creative American),
1287 1st Street
℄ 941/366-8111

Carmichaels
($$; award-winning American
and vegetarian), Palm Avenue,
Sarasota
℄ 941/951-1771

Cafe Lido
($$; International),
700 Benjamin Franklin Drive
℄ 941/388-2161

Colony Restaurant
($$$; award-winning fine dining
with American cuisine and
seafood, and a great wine list),
Colony Beach and Tennis
Resort, Longboat Key
℄ 941/383-5558

Columbia Restaurant
($$–$$$; award-winning
seafood and Spanish cuisine).
411, St Armands Circle
℄ 941/388-3987

Mirimar Restaurant
($$; Spanish, Cuban and
American), Sarasota Quay
℄ 941/954-3332

Ristorante Bellini
($$; Italian), 1551 Main Street,
Sarasota
℄ 941/365-7380

Sharky's On The Pier
($$; seafood), 1600 South
Harbor Drive, Venice
℄ 941/488-1456

Sunset Grille
($$; American/International),
4711 Gulf of Mexico Drive,
Longboat Key
℄ 941/383-2451

Charlotte Harbor

Port Charlotte stands at the head
of the huge natural Charlotte
Harbor and the mouth of the
Peace River. The community is
best known for its fishing; the
Charlotte Harbor Fishing Tour-
nament takes place here every
year in late winter. The waters
also provide great windsurfing,
and the harbour is the venue for
the annual Florida Invitational
Windsurfing Regatta which takes
place in October.

Punta Gorda, just across the
estuary of the Peace River, is the
county seat of Charlotte County,
and has a population of about
10,500. The old town has more
than 150 historic buildings. The
old city dock on the river is now
the busy little Fisherman's Vil-
lage, with a marina and shops.
There is also a 4 mile (6km) Art
Trail which starts at Fisherman's
Village and winds its way through
downtown, taking in a number of
art shops and galleries. The two-
day Florida International Air

Show is held each year at the end of March or in early spring.

King Fisher Cruise Lines in Fisherman's Village offers nature, sunset and fishing cruises to the offshore Gulf islands of Useppa, Cabbage Key and Cayo Costa. ✆ 941/639-0969

Charlotte Harbor Environmental Center lies to the southeast of Punta Gorda and covers 3,000 acres (1,200 hectares) of widely differing habitats. It is bordered to the north by Alligator Creek and to the west by Charlotte Harbor. There is a Visitor's Reception Center with a touch tank and there are a number of trails. This is a good place to watch basking gators, several species of turtle and tortoise, bobcats, the rare eastern indigo snake and a wealth of birdlife. Open: weekdays 8am–3pm during school term, and 8am–noon during holidays.

Lee Island Coast

The Lee Island Coast is one of the most exciting stretches along the Gulf Coast, with 590 miles (950km) of shoreline, 50 miles (81km) of white-sand beaches, and more than a hundred barrier and coastal islands, including stunning Sanibel Island.

The first settlers were Calusa Indians. Evidence of their culture dating back to 1150BC has been found, including ceremonial, burial and refuse shell-mounds at Mount Key, Pine Island, Cabbage Key and Useppa Island. The first European to visit the region was Juan Ponce de León, who left a stone marker on Pine Island in 1513. According to legend, the Spanish pirate José Gaspar had bases on Pine Island South and Sanibal, kept his female prisoners on Captiva and buried his treasure on Gasparilla Island. Rather than be taken prisoner by the US Navy in 1821, he is said to have wrapped himself in chains, jumped into the sea and drowned. It was in the same year that Spain sold Florida to the US government for $13 million. Forty-four years later, on 20 February 1865, the southernmost land battle of the Civil War was fought in Fort Myers, with both sides claiming victory. North Fort Myers celebrates this event annually with a battle re-enactment as part of its Cracker Festival.

Lee County was founded in 1887 and named after General Robert E Lee, although he never visited the area. It has only been in the last hundred years or so that the area has been settled, fishing being one of the main draws. The sport of tarpon fishing originated at Pine Island Sound in the late 1880s, while Boca Grande Pass, the opening between Cayo Costa and Gasparilla Island, is regarded as the 'Tarpon Fishing Capital of the World'.

There is still great year-round fishing for a wide range of inshore and offshore species. The best inshore species are snook, redfish, spotted seatrout, sheepshead, jack crevalle and mangrove snapper. Offshore species include shark, grouper, bonito, barracuda, permit, blackfin tuna, cobia, and Spanish and king mackerel. Bass, crappie, blue gill, shellcrackers, catfish and oscars are the main freshwater species. Expect to pay $25 for a half-day and $40 for a full day on a fishing party boat, or $150 for a half-day and up to $400 for a full day on your own charter boat.

While fishing attracted the visitors, cattle ranching was the main land-based activity. Among the first settlers, however, were flower-growers from Holland who turned Fort Myers into the 'Gladioli Capital of the World'. Prolific inventor Thomas Edison, who was credited with more than 1,000 patents, had his winter home in Fort Myers, now preserved as a museum. Edison's neighbours included Henry Ford and the tyre manufacturer Harvey Firestone.

Today, the Lee Island Coast is famous for its beaches, some of them the best in the world for shelling, and as one of the top ten tourist destinations in the United States. Among its beauty spots and beaches it can count Sanibel Island, Captiva, Fort Myers Beach (on Estero Island), Bonita Springs and Beach, Fort Myers, Pine Island, Cape Coral, Lehigh Acres, Boca Grande (on Gasparilla Island), North Fort Myers, Cabbage Key, Useppa Island, Cayo Costa State Island Preserve and North Captiva Island.

The coast is a major winter destination, with rates from the end of April to December generally significantly lower, so it offers great value to summer visitors. There are more than 20,000 rooms, ranging from deluxe resorts, hotels and motels to beachside cottages and condominiums. There are also more than 3,500 campsites and forty fully equipped RV parks, plus an extra seventeen RV parks with additional tent camping.

The area boasts ninety-five golf courses and fifty-eight marinas, with fifteen of these offering boat rentals and charters. It is even possible to sail a boat from Fort Myers right across the state to the Atlantic Coast at Palm Beach by travelling along the Caloosahatchee River and Okeechobee Waterway. Lee County also boasts one of the world's largest populations of bottlenose dolphins and West Indian manatees.

Southwest Florida International Airport, to the south-east of Fort Myers, serves Lee, Charlotte and Collier counties. It opened in 1984, and receives flights from most domestic carriers and several international charter operations. Another airport, the Page Field Executive Airport, is located near downtown Fort Myers.

Cayo Costa State Park, at the mouth of Charlotte Harbor, has 7 miles (11km) of fabulous white-sand beaches backed by pine forest, oak hammocks and mangrove swamps. It is one of the older barrier reefs along the coast, and can only be reached by private boat or ferry. There is great swimming and shelling here – it is possible to find up to sixty different types of shell on a good day, which are usually intact as there are no offshore reefs to break them up as they are washed in. The island also teems with wildlife, and facilites include primitive camping and rental cabins. To get there, take Highway 78 to Pine Island, turning north on Stringfellow Road to Bokeelia. Park at the Four Winds Marina, from where you catch the ferry. ✆ 941/964-0375.

Cabbage Key lies just to the east of Cayo Costa. One of its most popular attractions is the historic Cabbage Key Inn, which was built on an ancient Indian shell mound. The walls of the restaurant are papered with more than $20,000-worth of autographed $1 bills. The tradition is said to have started when a fishermen pinned a dollar bill to the wall so that he could afford a cold beer the next time he called in. The inn was built by playwright Mary Roberts Rinehart and her son in 1938, and has six rustic guest rooms, guest cottages, a marina, nature trails and a wooden water tower which can be climbed for views over Pine Island Sound. The inn stands at Channel Marker 60 on the Intracoastal Waterway. ✆ 941/283-2278.

Neighbouring **Useppa Island**, inhabited by Calusa Indians as long ago as 5000BC, is said to have been named by pirate José Gaspar after Josefa, a Mexican princess he captured and then fell in love with. Barron Collier bought the island in 1912 and founded the exclusive Izaak Walton Anglers Club of Useppa, which attracted the rich and famous, including the DuPonts, the Roosevelts and Mae West. Apart from its tarpon fishing, it offered tennis courts, a swimming-pool, an imported white-sand beach and an illegal casino. This elegant, private resort is still a sportsman's mecca today. ✆ 941/283-1061. The Useppa displays exhibits dating back 12,000 years. Open: Tuesday to Sunday 1pm–3pm. ✆ 941/283-9600.

Boca Grande, on Gasparilla Island, offers a taste of old Florida and is connected to the mainland by a short causeway near Punta Gorda. The settlement was established by the DuPont family in the late 1800s, and the small fishing town has changed little over the years, retaining its yesteryear charm despite the development

Above: Fort Myers Beach **Below:** Canoe Escape take you to where its very peaceful

that has sprung up around it. It has interesting shops and cosy restaurants, waterside accommodation and beautiful beaches. The surrounding waters offer some of the world's best tarpon fishing. Sights include the Gasparilla Inn, built in 1912 as a stylish resort for the rich and famous, the Fugates department store, which opened in 1915 and has been run by the same family ever since, and the Old Theater Arcade, which was built in the 1920s to raise money for the island's first medical clinic. Historic Banyan Street is lined with banyan trees originally planted by Peter Vradley, the former president of the Charlotte Harbor and Northern Railroad, while the Coast Guard Lighthouse at the southern tip of the island was built in 1927. This is a great spot for fishing and picnicking, but swimming is not recommended as there are strong currents off shore.

Cape Coral lies on the northern side of the Caloosahatchee River estuary and boasts more canals than the Italian city of Venice. Its beaches and parks include: Lake Kennedy Park, with a playground, boat ramp, fishing and toilets; Veteran's Memorial Park, with a games area, a playground, an open pavilion, picnic areas and toilets; Four Freedoms Park, with a recreation centre, a playground, an amphitheatre, a picnic area and fishing; Jaycee Park, with a jogging track and exercise stations, picnic pavilions and toilets; Jason Verdow Memorial Park, with little-league baseball fields, picnic spots and toilets; Pelican Sports Complex, with a large games area, a playground and toilets; J Chandler Burton Memorial Park, with a games area, tennis courts, a playground and toilets; Guiffrida Park, with picnic and barbecue areas, pavilions and a playground; Caloosa Park, with a games area and toilets; and Koza-Saladino Park, with little-league baseball fields, toilets and picnic tables. The main shopping area is Coralwood Mall, on Del Prado Boulevard.

Fort Myers is the main city along the south-west Florida coast, and is packed with historic sites, fine old homes and museums. In the mid-1800s there were many Seminole Indians (Seminole is the Creek word for 'free' or 'runaway') and fugitive slaves in the area, and in 1865 Fort Myers (formerly Fort Harvie) was reopened as a Union fort, where the 2nd US Union Federalists Color Troops were stationed. The first school for black children was established in 1887, and the Dunbar Community School still serves the Dunbar community today. Nelson Tillis, a farmer and fishing guide, is reputed to have been the first black settler in Fort Myers.

Today, Fort Myers is known as the 'City of Palms'; McGregor Boulevard (originally a cattle trail), running through the city, is lined with towering royal palms, the first 200 of which were imported from Cuba by Thomas Edison. There are many fine homes lying between the boulevard and the Caloosahatchee River, while a 1926 statue of a Grecian maiden stands in the area known as Edison Park. The maiden, a local landmark, was originally to have been naked, but the resulting controversy was ended when Mrs Edison ruled that she should be modestly draped. The Thomas Edison Congregational Church also stands in the Edison Park sub-division, as do many magnificent old homes, these varying in architectural style from Mediterranean Revival to neoclassical.

Fort Myers Sights

The **Thomas Edison Winter Home and Museum** (2350 McGregor Boulevard), one of the city's major attractions, was Edison's winter home for forty-six years. The house is set in a 14 acre (6 hectare) riverfront estate and was built in 1866. Edison is credited with 1,097 patents for his inventions, which ranged from light-bulbs and phonographs to cement and a natural rubber. Outside, his experimental botanical garden is considered unique because each specimen was included for its scientific value. The huge banyan

tree in the garden was a gift to Edison from industrialist Harvey Firestone. The tree is the largest banyan specimen in the United States, its aerial roots having a circumference of more than 400ft (122m). There are tours of the inventor's home, laboratory, botanical garden and museum throughout the day. Open: weekdays and Saturday 9am–5.30pm and Sunday noon–5.30pm. ✆ 941/334-3614

The **Henry Ford-Biggar Home** (2400 McGregor Boulevard) was the winter home of Edison's close friend, Henry Ford. Ford was a frequent house guest of Edison until he and his wife Clara had their own bungalow-style home built next door in 1916, which they called Mangoes. Open: daily for tours. ✆ 941/334-3614

On the other side of town is the historic Georgian Revival-style **Murphy-Burroughs Home**, built in 1901 by wealthy cattleman John Murphy. He visited the area in the 1890s, bought a plot of land with 450ft (137m) of river frontage for $3,500 in 1899 and then constructed his home, triggering a turn-of-the-century residential building boom in the process. Open: for tours on the hour Monday to Friday 10am–3pm. ✆ 941/332-6125

Other historic buildings in the downtown area include **The Veranda** (corner of Broadway and Second Street), a turn-of-the-century boarding house, which is now a popular bar and restaurant. The walls are covered with photographs and memorabilia of old Fort Myers.

The **Fort Myers Historical Museum** is housed in the restored Peck Street Depot (2300 Peck Street), which operated as a railway station for sixty-seven years until 1971. It has displays and exhibits from the now extinct Calusa Indian civilization, as well as items from the Seminole and Miccosukee tribes that date right up to the present day. The first gift to the museum was the Ethel Cooper glass collection of 1,000 pieces, although only a portion is on display. Open: from November to April Monday to Saturday 9am–4.30pm and Sunday 1pm–5pm, and from May to October weekdays only 9am–4.30pm. © 941/332-5955

The **Seminole Gulf Railway** offers the chance of a ride through Florida's subtropical terrain aboard an elegant old-fashioned dining car or carriage. Trains leave from the Metro Mall Railway Station on Colonial Boulevard, and there are dinner, murder-mystery and sightseeing excursions. © 941/275-8487

Fort Myers Culture and Shopping

The city has a rich cultural life, based particularly around the William R Frizzell Cultural Center. © 941/939-2787

The **Arcade Theater** is a renovated Victoria playhouse in the Harborside Complex, staging theatre, dance and music (© 941/338-2244), while the **Barbara B Mann Performing Arts Hall**, on the campus of the University of South Florida, features national Broadway productions, big-name entertainers, dance and music year round. © 941/481-4849. The **Broadway Palm Dinner Theater**, on Colonial Boulevard, offers Broadway-style shows over dinner (© 941/278-4422), and the **Cultural Park Theater**, which opened in 1991 in neighbouring Cape Coral, has a wide range of artistic offerings. © 941/574-0465

The main shopping areas in Fort Myers include Historic Downtown First Street, Edison Mall, Bell Tower Shops, Royal Palm Square, Metro Mall, Sanibel Factory Outlets and Fleamasters Fleamarket.

Beyond Fort Myers

The **Lee County Nature Centre and Planetarium** (Ortiz Boulevard, south-east of Fort Myers) has a native aviary, a boardwalk through a natural swamp and several exhibits in its main building. The planetarium opened in 1986 and offers day and evening presentations, laser shows and special programmes. © 941/275-3435

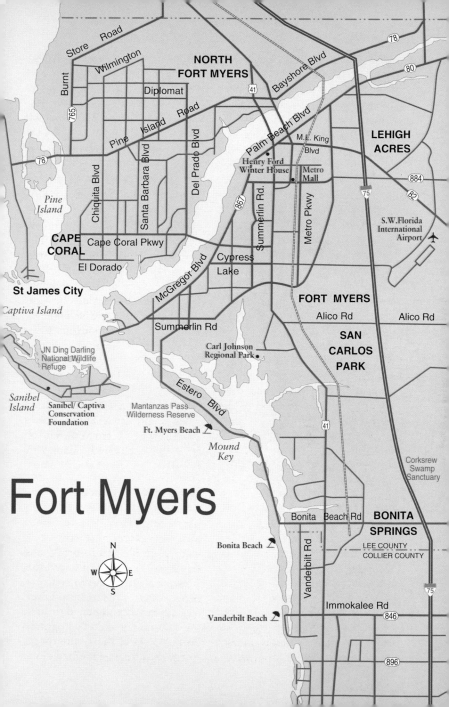

Fort Myers Beach (Estero Island) is a popular family destination as its gently sloping shoreline, soft sand and warm, clear waters make it one of the world's safest beaches. Estero Bay is usually packed with commercial shrimp and fishing boats during the winter, and you can buy seafood fresh from the docks. There is a wealth of watersports, and the marinas offer boating and fishing charters. Local beaches and parks include Carl E Johnson Park and Lover's Key, Bowditch Point Regional Park, Lynn Hall Memorial Park, Montanzas Pass Wilderness Reserve and Mound Key, while the main shopping areas are the Seafarers Village Shopping Mall, Times Square and Santini Plaza.

The **Ostego Bay Foundation** is a marine research and educational facility off Fort Myers Beach on San Carlos Island, under the Skybridge at Gulf Star Marina. It has a Marine Science Center, a touch tank and aquariums, and gives lectures on the endangered loggerhead turtle. Open: Saturday 10am–4pm and Sunday 1pm–4pm. ℡ 941/765-8101

The **Mantanzas Pass Wilderness Reserve** on Estero Island has 40 acres (16 hectares) of live oak hammock and 4,000ft (1,220m) of mangrove shoreline, all of which can explored by an elevated boardwalk. Open: dawn–dusk. Admission is free. Off the southern tip of Estero Island, and only accessible by boat, is **Mound Key**, which is largely constructed from shells that were discarded by Calusa Indians many centuries ago.

The **Carl Johnson Regional Park** lies south of Fort Myers Beach. Take Highway 865 south across the causeway over Big Carlos Pass for the park entrance at Lover's Key on Black Island. The park has two distinct ecosystems: mangrove estuary and sandy barrier island. You can walk or take a tram through the mangroves to the tidal bay, crossing Oyster Bay to one of the most private public beaches you are ever likely to find. The unspoilt, secluded beach is great for picnicking, shelling and fishing. Oysters live among the mangrove roots and provide food for birds and raccoons. ℡ 941/432-2000

Six Mile Cypress Slough is a relatively new nature reserve which acts as a natural corridor for wildlife from the interior to the Estero Bay. It covers 2,000 acres (800 hectares) of wetlands, and animal life includes raccoons, squirrels, skinks, bobcats, otters and white-tailed deer. You can also see gators, vultures, bald eagles, hawks and many wetland birds and waders. Take Colonial Boulevard in Fort Myers to Six Mile Parkway, then head south to Penzance Crossing. Turn left: the entrance is a couple of hundred metres along on the north side of the road. Opening times vary according to season. ☎ 941/432-2004.

Sanibel Island is an idyllic getaway reached by a toll causeway which helps to keep visitor numbers down. The island's beaches are consistently voted among the best in the world, and Sanibel is also world famous for its shelling and wildlife. More than 200 different types of shell have been found along its beaches. Sanibel has banned live shelling, and Lee County encourages shell-seekers to pick up treasures which have washed up on shore. The island is also one of the best places to watch spectacular sunsets, while Sanibel Lighthouse is one of the most photographed landmarks on the Gulf Coast. It was built at the southern tip of the island in 1884, and stands between two stilt houses, typical of turn-of-the-century Floridian architecture.

Periwinkle Way is the main thoroughfare, and on either side the lush tropical vegetation is interspersed with interesting shops, galleries and fine restaurants. The best way to get around the island is to hire a bicycle from one of the many outlets. Shopping centres to explore include Chadwick's Square, Periwinkle Place, the Islander Shopping Center and the Village Shopping Center. Bailey's Shopping Centre is home to the first store opened on the island (in the late 1800s), and is still run by the Bailey family today. The Old Schoolhouse Theater, formerly a one-room schoolhouse built in 1894, now offers a cosy theatre venue for a mix of professional productions and community theatre. ☎ 941/472-6862 The Pirate Playhouse (Periwinkle Way) stages major productions and attracts big-name stars to a professional yet intimate venue where no seat is more than 15ft (5m) from the stage. ☎ 941/472-0006

The **JN 'Ding' Darling National Wildlife Refuge** is one of Florida's best wildlife spots and occupies some 5,400 acres (2,160 hectares) on the north side of Sanibel Island. It was established as the Sanibel National Wildlife Refuge in 1945, was renamed after Pulitzer prize-winning cartoonist Jay Norwood 'Ding' Darling in 1967, and was formally dedicated in 1978. Darling was also the first environmentalist to hold a presidential cabinet post (in Franklin Roosevelt's administration). There are driving, walking and cycling trails, and you can hire a canoe or kayak and paddle your way along the coast through the tiny offshore mangrove islands. The Commodore Creek Canoe Trail (named after an early homesteader) meanders for 1.5 miles (2km) through the mangroves, and there is also the 4 mile (6km) Buck Key Canoe Trail. The 5 mile (8km) scenic drive can be driven, cycled or walked. The refuge has more than 300 species of birds, more than fifty species of

Above: End of the day at Naples *Below:* Gator Xing. Look out for the gators, especially after dark!

amphibian and thirty-five species of mammal. Sunrise, sunset and low tide are the best wildlife viewing times. Open: every day except Friday sun-up–sundown. ℂ 941/472-1100

The **Sanibel-Captiva Conservation Foundation** is a delightful nature centre covering 1,100 acres (440 hectares) just south of the island's main road. There are more than 4 miles (6.5km) of trails through very diverse habitats, an observation tower and interpretive signs. ℂ 941/472-2329

Other sights on Sanibel include the Bailey-Matthews Shell Museum (Sanibel–Captiva road) the only dedicated seashell museum in the US (Open: Tuesday to Sunday 10am–4pm. ℂ 941/395-2233), and CROW (Care and Rehabilitation of Wildlife; just west of Rabbit Road), a sanctuary for sick, injured and orphaned wildlife. Open: Monday to Friday for tours at 11am, and on Sunday at 1pm. ℂ 941/472-3644. The best beaches on Sanibel and Captiva are Bowman's Beach (on Bowman's Beach Road), Sanibel Lighthouse, Gulfside Park (on Sanibel's south coast) and pristine Turner Beach, which runs between the two islands.

Captiva Island is the northern neighbour of Sanibel Island and is linked to it by a short bridge. It is said that the main attractions of Captiva are that it has none, although both islands are popular tourist resorts with great beaches, abundant wildlife, fine private homes and many restaurants. Both islands are also world famous for shell-collecting, and this pastime is so popular that the locals have given names to the shelling postures, such as the 'Captiva Crouch' and the 'Sanibel Stoop'. Among the many rare shells that can be found on the beaches are brown speckled junonia, sculpted lion's paw, golden olive, golden tulip and Scotch bonnet. Captiva is ideal if you just want to enjoy the beaches and warm waters. It was also here that Anne Morrow Lindbergh, wife of the famous aviator, wrote her best-selling love letter 'A Gift from the Sea'. North Captiva is usually fairly deserted.

The **Corkscrew Swamp Sanctuary**, just north of Naples, is the world's largest remaining subtropical bald cypress forest and is managed by the National Audubon Society. The 10,560 acre (4,224 hectare) reserve has trails through the pinelands, wet prairie, marsh and forest. It is noted for its rich bird- and animal life and for its spectacular wildflowers, especially orchids. There are gators, otters and turtles, and during the summer several hundred swallow-tailed kites take up residence. A free self-guided walk brochure is available from the visitor centre. Open: daily. ℂ 941/348-9151.

Bonita Beach marks the southern boundary of the Lee Island Coast and has wonderful beaches. Boardwalks lead to the pristine beach at Bonita Beach Park to protect the sea oats, sand dunes and coastal vegetation, and there is a gazebo, picnic tables, toilets, changing rooms and outdoor showers. There is also parking and disabled access. Lee Tran buses and trolleys offer a free service to the beach.

Bonita Springs, just inland off Interstate 75, is home to the **Koreshan State Historic Site**, which commemorates a rather eccentric religious sect that was founded in the 1890s. Members of the sect believed that the world was a hollow globe, with mankind living on the inner surface and gazing into a universe contained within the sphere. The Koreshan Unity was established by Dr Cyrus Teed, a Union Army doctor, who had a vision telling him to change his name to Koresh and move with his followers to south-western Florida. They planned to build a huge city to house the 10 million followers they expected to attract. Things did not work out as planned, however, and at the peak of its popularity the settlement had a population of only 250. Of the original sixty buildings, sixteen remain, including the open-air theatre and Teed's original home. There is also a nature trail, a boat ramp, fresh- and saltwater fishing and camping. Open: daily 8am–5pm; the site is being restored. ✆ 941/992-0311. The **Koreshan Unity Foundation and Library** lies across the park at 8661 Corkscrew Road. ✆ 941/992-2184.

Springs Plaza is the main shopping area for Bonita Springs, with boutiques, restaurants, speciality shops and a twenty-four-hour grocery store. On the sports side, the Naples-Fort Myers Greyhound Track at Bontia Beach Road holds races nightly from Tuesday to Saturday, with matinée racing on Wednesday, Saturday and Sunday. ✆ 941/992-2411

Lee Island Coast Restaurants

Brigands
($$; seafood and steaks), Cape Coral Parkway W, Cape Coral ✆ 941/540-HOOK

Casa de Guerrera
($$; Mexican), 2225 First Street, Fort Myers ✆ 941/332-4674

Jacaranda
($$; seafood and pasta), Periwinkle Way, Sanibel ✆ 941/472-1771

Mel's Diner
($$; American), 4820 South Cleveland Avenue, Fort Myers

Old Captiva House
($$–$$$; award-winning fine

dining), next to Tween Waters
Inn, Captiva Island
✆ 941/472-5161

Origami
($$; Japanese and Korean),
13300 South Cleveland Avenue,
Fort Myers
✆ 941/482-2126

Stooges Eatery
($; American), Cape Coral
Parkway, Cape Coral
✆ 941/549-9000

The Veranda
($$–$$$; award-winning fine
dining), corner of Second Street
and Broadway, Fort Myers
✆ 941/332-2065

Naples

Naples boasts more than 40 miles
(64km) of fabulous beaches, and
has come a long way in the last
hundred years or so. When it was
founded in 1885, the only way to
reach the settlement was by boat;
Naples Pier is a relic from those
days. Today, Naples is growing
fast and seems to be rivalling fash-
ionable and up-market Palm
Beach across the state on the At-
lantic coast. There are expensive
shops and boutiques, galleries and
eateries along Fifth Avenue, and
other shopping opportunities at
Third Street, The Avenues in Old
Naples, Tin City, The Village on

Venetian Bay and the waterside
shops at Pelican Bay. However, it
is Naples' beaches that attract the
visitors, as well as the shelling and
wildlife.

To the north lies the **Delnor
Wiggins Pass State Recreation
Area** and, in North Naples, the
Clam Pass Sanctuary, both of
which are rated among the top
twenty US beaches. To the south
is **Rookery Bay**, noted for its
prolific wildlife and mangrove
swamps.

The area's best beaches include
Delnor Wiggins Pass State Rec-
reation Area, Barefoot Beach,
Cochatchee River Park, Clam
Pass Park, Lowdermill Park and
Tigertail Beach. Naples offers a
wide range of outdoor activities,
from golf to fishing, sailing
and air-boat rides. In addition,
swamp-buggy races are usually
held during the last week of Octo-
ber off Country Road 951. This
sport has been popular in the Na-
ples area for almost fifty years.

Naples Sights

The **Philharmonic Center for the
Arts** (Pelican Bay Boulevard) has a
year-round programme. ✆ 941/
597-1900

Collier County Museum (cor-
ner of Highway 41E and Airport
Road) traces the history of the
area, from the Calusi Indians to
the present day. The grounds con-
tain the reconstruction of a

Seminole Indian Village. Open: Monday to Friday 9am–5pm. ℗ 941/774-8476

The **Conservancy and Naples Nature Center** (1450 Merrihue Drive) features wildlife exhibits, an animal clinic, a natural science museum, a marine aquarium, a touch tank, an outdoor aviary and nature trails. Open: Monday to Saturday 9.30am–4.30pm and Sunday 1–5pm from January to March, weekdays and Saturday only from April to September, and weekdays only during the rest of the year. ℗ 941/775-8569

Teddy Bear Museum of Naples (2511 Pine Ridge Road off Exit 16 of Interstate 75) has more than 1,500 teddy bears on display and puts on changing exhibitions. Open: Wednesday to Saturday 10am–5pm and Sunday 1pm–5pm. ℗ 941/598-2711

Jungle Larry's Zoological Park (at the Caribbean Gardens on Goodlette Road, off Highway 41) has self-guided walking trails through its 52 acre (84 hectare) grounds, where wild animals and birds live in a jungle setting. There are also boat rides, a petting zoo and animal shows. Open: daily 9.30am–5.30pm. ℗ 941/262-5409

The **Naples Depot Civic and Cultural Centre** (Fifth Avenue S) is housed in the renovated 1927 railway station, and displays railway memorabilia and art exhibits.

Preceding Page: An Everglades airboat

Open: Monday to Friday 10am–4pm. ℗ 941/262-1776

The **Briggs Nature Center** is part of the 9,200 acre (3,680 hectare) Rookery Bay National Estuarine Research Reserve. There are trails through the marshes, mangroves and coastal hammocks, an observation deck and ranger-led pontoon boat tours between December and May that deal with bird-watching, beachcombing and marine ecology. Canoe trips are also available. Apart from the rich birdlife, the wealth of wildflowers attracts large numbers of butterflies; there is a special butterfly garden near the car park. Bottlenose dolphins and manatees can be spotted offshore. The centre is reached by taking Highway 951 towards Marco Island, and then turning right onto Shell Island Road for 1 mile (1.6km) to the entrance.

Naples Restaurants

Alice Sweetwaters
($$; American and seafood),
Airport Road,
South Naples
℗ 941/793-3700

Bayside
($$–$$$; seafood),
Gulfshore Boulevard
℗ 941/649-5552

Chef's Garden
($$–$$$; American), 1300

Third Street
℡ 941/262-5500

Dock at Crayton Cove
($$; seafood), 12th Avenue S
℡ 941/263-9940

Fernandez the Bull
($$; Cuban), North Tamiami
Drive
℡ 941/263-2996

Fifth Avenue Deli
($; German and deli), 5th
Avenue
℡ 941/262-4106

Lafite
($$$; fine American), 475
Seagate Drive
℡ 941/597-3232

L'Auberge
($$; French), Fifth Street
℡ 941/261-8148

Michelbob's
($$; award-winning steaks and
ribs), Highway 41 and 103rd
Avenue, North Naples
℡ 941/594-PORK. Also at 371
Airport Road, Naples
℡ 941/643-2877

Loquats
($$; German),
North Tamiami Drive
℡ 941/597-4871

Riverwalk
($$; seafood), 4th Avenue S
℡ 941/263-2734

The English Restaurant
($$; famous for fish and chips),
2408 Linwood Avenue, Naples
℡ 941/774-2408

Villa Pescatore
($$–$$$; Italian and seafood),
North Tamiami Drive
℡ 941/597-8119.

Marco Island Restaurants

Bavarian Inn
($$; German), Winterberry
Drive. ℡ 941/394-7233

Sandcastles
($$; American), South Collier
Boulevard
℡ 941/394-5000

Snook Inn ($$; seafood and
Continental), 1215 Bald Eagle
Drive
℡ 941/394-3313

TenThousand Islands and the Everglades

Marco Island stands at the northern tip of Ten Thousand Islands and is reached by taking State Roads 92 or 951 from Highway 41. The island, once a small fishing community, is now an up-market resort with great beaches and a wealth of watersports, including good surfing. The beaches are also popular with shell-collectors. Marco Island Trolley Tours offers guided tours of the island, including early Calusa Indian sites. Open: tours daily 8.45am–5pm. ℂ 941/394-1600

The 61,962 acre (24,784 hectare) **Fakahatchee Strand State Preserve**, just north of Everglades City, is a huge forested swamp with great mangrove estuaries reaching out to Ten Thousand Islands. It is home to North America's largest stand of native royal palms, as well as many species of ferns, orchids and air plants. The diverse habitats, including lakes, marle prairies, hammocks and cypress wood swamps, are refuges for the endangered Florida panther, black bear, Everglades mink and wood stork. You can also see gators, turtles, river otters, white-tailed deer, raccoons, opossums, bobcats and huge numbers of birds. There are many marked trails along logging roads, and maps are available from the ranger station on Jane's Scenic Drive.

The small community of **Everglades City** (population 300) lies at the north-western corner of the huge national park and is a popular starting point for fishing trips and excursions into the park. It is about 5 miles (8km) south of the Tamiami Trail on Highway 29 and is the best place from which to explore the Ten Thousand Islands, only accessible by boat or canoe. You can spot dolphins, manatees, gators, rays, sharks and scores of species of birds, such as spoonbills, ibises, herons, egrets and ospreys. Maps and backcountry permits for boats and canoes are available from the visitor's centre, and you can also sign up for ranger-led tours (✆ 941/695-2591 or 1-800-445-7724 for schedules and reservations). Also of interest is Eden of the Everglades, on State Road 29, which has an elevated boardwalk through the mangrove forest and offers pontoon-boat trips around Ten Thousand Islands (✆ 941/695-2800). The wooden EJ Hamilton Observation Tower (always open) is located to the south on State Road 29, and offers spectacular views of the islands if you can climb the 180 steps.

Finally, there is the **Everglades National Park**, which covers more than 1 million acres (400,000 hectares) at the southern tip of Florida and forms one of the world's great natural areas. The western part of the park runs out into the Gulf of Mexico in a maze of mangrove swamps, small islands and hummocks, these supporting an amazing wealth of wildlife. There are several entrances to the park; from the Gulf Coast you can gain access via Everglades City or Flamingo to the south, from where there is a 38 mile (61km) road to the park's headquarters and main visitor centre. There are lots of walking and canoeing trails, but make sure you have a good map and do not stray off the route as it is easy to get lost. Boat tours and canoe and bike rentals are available in **Flamingo**, while nearby Eco Pond is a good place for watching birds, especially herons, egrets and ibises.

ACCOMMODATION

Hotels and Motels

There is a huge range of hotel and motel accommodation to choose from all along the Gulf Coast. Categories range from luxury to basic, and there is always something to suit your taste and pocket.

Many modern hotels and motels usually offer two double beds in each room, and as you pay for the room, this can work out very reasonably if you are travelling with family or close friends. Rooms are also much larger than in Europe, and can often accommodate an extra single bed or cot, which will be provided for a small additional fee as long as adequate notice is given. Rooms usually have en suite bathroom and telephone, air-conditioning and cable/satellite television as standard. Rooms in older establishments tend to be smaller and often offer rooms with just a single or double bed. Because competition is intense, prices are generally lower than comparable accommodation elsewhere, even in the high season, and there are usually added incentives to tempt you. These can range from free breakfasts to free watersports and boat trips.

Prices vary according to season and standards of service offered. Most hotel chains offer vouchers which, if pre-paid, give substantial discounts, so it is worth checking with your travel company. Before buying vouchers, however, make sure the hotel offers the standard of service you require. There are also substantial discounts for senior citizens and members of the American Automobile Association (AAA), which may be worth joining even if you don't live in the United States but make frequent trips there.

If visiting during the peak season (between Christmas and May), it is advisable to reserve accommodation. At other times, you may want to cruise around, and hunt out the best bargains. All motels and hotels clearly advertise their prices and any perks on offer, and you can always pop in and check out the room before deciding. If you feel up to it, you can always haggle over the price to see if you can get a few dollars knocked off for a stay of several nights or payment in cash.

Many hotels and large motels have their own restaurants, and will usually offer American Plan (AP), equivalent to full board with all meals provided, or Modified Plan (MP), which offers accommodation plus breakfast and dinner. If the establishment has no restaurant, coffee is usually available in the lobby with free doughnuts offered in lieu of breakfast, and in any case there will be a good selection of restaurants and fast-food outlets near by. Ice machines and soft-drinks vending machines are generally also provided.

Given the huge choice of accommodation, the selection below represents only a small proportion of what is available.

Pensacola

Hampton Inn $-$$
7330 Plantation Road
✆ 904-477-3333

Pensacola Grand Hotel $$-$$$
200 East Gregory St.
✆ 904-433-3336
Lovely hotel built around the converted 1912 railway station.

Residence Inn by Marriott $$
7230 Plantation Rd
✆ 904-479-1000

Emerald Coast area

Destin
Howard Johnson $$
713 Highway 98 East
✆ 904-837-5455

Frangista Beach Inn $$-$$$
4150 Old Highway 98 East
✆ 904-654-5501

Sandestin $$-$$$
5500 US 98 East
✆ 904-267-8000

Fort Walton
Marina Bay Resort $-$$
80 Miracle Strip Py
✆ 904-244-5132

Sea Isle Motel $-$$
1214 Highway 98 East
✆ 904-243-5563

Sheraton; Four Pointsby $$-$$$
1325 Miracle Strip Parkway
✆ 904-243-8116

Panama City

Best Western Bayside Inn $$
711 West Beach Drive
✆ 904-763-4622

Comfort Inn $$
1013 East 23rd Street
Conveniently located near beach, shops and restaurants, with 105 rooms. ✆ 904-769-6969

Panama City Beach

Impala Motel $-$$
17751 Front Beach Rd
✆ 904-234-6462

La Brisa Motor Inn $
9424 Front Beach Road
A 60 room inn on the beach xlose to all amenities.
✆ 904-235-1122

Regency Towers $$-$$$
5801 Thomas Dr
✆ 904-234-3533

Fact File

Tallahassee

Courtyard by Marriott $$-$$$
1018 Apalachee Py
© 904-222-8822

Radisson Hotel Tallahassee $$
415 North Monroe St
© 904-224-6000

Cedar Keys to Tarpon Springs

Best Western Tahitian Resort $$
2337 US 19, Holiday
© 813-937-4121

Days Inn $-$$
11736 US 19, Port Richey
© 813-863-1502

Ramada Inn Bayside $$
5015 US 19, New Port Richey
© 813-849-8551

St Petersburg and Clearwater

Bayborough House $$
1719 Beach Drive, St.
Petersburg © 813-823-4955

Belleview Mido Resort Hotel $$-$$$
25 Belleview Boulevard,
Clearwater © 813-442-6171

Best Western Clearwater Central $$
21338 US 19 North, Clearwater
© 813-799-1565

Best Western Sirata Beach Resort $$-$$$
5390 Gulf Boulevard,
St. Petersburg Beach
© 813-367-2771

Radisson Suites Resort $$-$$$
1201 Gulf Boulevard,
Sand Key
© 813-596-1100

Rodeway Inn Central $-$$
20967 US 19 North, Clearwater
© 813-797-8504

Renaissance Vinoy Resort
$$$, 501 Fifth Avenue NE,
St. Petersburg
© 813-894-1000
A grand hotel which opened in
1925 and still offers luxury at a
price.

Super 8 $-$$
22950 US 19 North, Clearwater
© 813-799-2678

Tampa

Courtyard by Marriott $$
3805 West Cypress St
© 813-874-0555

Hyatt Regency Tampa
$$-$$$
2 Tampa City Centre
© 813-225-1234

Bradenton and Sarasota

Anna Maria Island Club $$$
2600 Gulf Drive North,
Anna Maria Island
© 941-778-4800

Above: *Relaxing on the miles of soft white sandy beaches that are typical of Florida*

Fact File

Aquarius Beach Resort
$$-$$$
105 39th Street, Holmes Beach
© 941-778-7477

Bay Motel **$**
8110 North Trail,
Sarasota
© 941-335-8861

Quality Inn and Suites **$$**
2303 1st Street East,
Bradenton
© 941-747-6465

Harbour Villa Club **$$$**
615 Dream Island Road,
Longboat Key
© 941-383-9544

Howard Johnson Inn **$$**
6511 14th Street West,
Bradenton
© 941-756-8399

Sleep Inn **$$**
900 University Parkway,
Sarasota
© 941-359-5775

Fort Myers, Naples and Area

Best Western Naples Inn **$$**
2329 North US41
© 941-261-1148

Casa Ybel Resort **$$$**
2255 West Gulf Drive,
Sanibel Island
© 941-642-2400

**Captain's Table
Lodge and Villas** **$$**
102 East Broadway,
Everglades,
© 941-695-4211

Lani Kai Island Resort **$$$**
1400 Estero Boulevard,
Fort Myers Beach
© 941-463-3111

**Best Western Sanibel Island
Beach Resort** **$$-$$$**
3287 West Gulf Drive,
Sanibel Island
© 941-472-1700

Vanderbilt Inn **$$**
11000 Gulf Shore Drive,
North Naples
© 941-597-3151

Condominiums

A condominium, or condo, is an apartment of several rooms.
There may be just a few condos in the building or hundreds in a
high-rise block. Many people from out of state buy condos as an
investment and as a summer holiday home, renting them out
through agents when they are not there. Condos are available to
rent for a week or longer. They offer more space and privacy
than a hotel or motel room, and for larger groups they work out
much cheaper.

Resorts

These usually consist of a large hotel built in its own grounds,
often on the beach, which offers first-class accommodation,

food, entertainment and a wide range of facilities. The latter may include land- and water-based sports, boat cruises, sea fishing and a dive centre.

Guesthouses and Bed and Breakfasts
These are worth hunting out if you want a taste of real Florida living. They are often more expensive than a cheap motel or hotel, but they do allow you to stay in a family home. Local tourist offices have lists of guesthouses (also known as boarding houses) and homes offering bed and breakfast accommodation.

Rental Homes
There are many private homes in Florida available to rent. The standard of property varies enormously, and this is reflected in the rental price. Most homes are furnished to high standards and have air-conditioning, and many also have their own swimming-pools. They may also come with housekeeping services. For larger families and groups, the cost of renting a three- or four-bedroom house (or even two houses near each other) is significantly cheaper than comparable hotel accommodation, plus you have the added bonus of more space, privacy and your own pool.

For camping and recreational vehicle (RV) information, see page 134.

AIRPORTS AND AIRLINES

Airports

Charlotte County Airport
✆ 941/639-1101
Destin-Fort Walton
✆ 904/651-7160
Hernando County Airport
✆ 352/799-7275
Naples Municipal Airport
✆ 941/643-0733
Panama City-Bay County International Airport
✆ 904/763-6751
Pensacola Regional Airport
✆ 904/435-1746
St Petersburg-Clearwater International Airport
✆ 813/531-1451

Sarasota-Bradenton International Airport
✆ 941/359-5200
Southwest Florida International Airport, Fort Myers
✆ 941/768-1000
Tallahassee Regional Airport
✆ 904/891-7800
Tampa International Airport
✆ 813/870-8700
Venice Municipal Airport
✆ 941/485-9293

Fact File

Airlines

American Airlines
✆ 1-800-433-7300

ComAir (Delta Connection)
✆ 1-800-354-9822
USAirways
✆ 1-800-428-4322

ALCOHOL

You must be twenty-one years old to purchase or consume alcohol in Florida. Don't be offended if you are asked to prove your age. You can enter lounges and bars serving alcohol if you are eighteen, but you must stick to soft drinks.

BABYSITTING

Most hotels and resorts offer babysitting facilities, and there are also registered babysitting services that will send babysitters to your hotel room or villa, or take the children off your hands during the day. Most hotels and resorts also have special events and areas for children (infants to teens), with trained staff to supervise them.

BANKS

Banks are usually open Monday to Friday 9am–3pm, although some stay open to 4pm. Automatic tellers (cashpoint machines) offer twenty-four-hour access to cash and are widely available.

CAMPING AND RECREATIONAL VEHICLES

Caravans and motor homes (known as recreational vehicles, or RVs) pack the roads and campsites on the islands during the high season. RVs do offer high levels of accommodation, with the added advantage that if you get tired of the scenery you can always drive a few miles further up the road. Campsites and RV parks, which are found along the length of Highway 1, are equipped to a high standard, with electricity and water hook-ups, on-site shops, restaurants, bars, pools and club houses, as well as many other facilities. Off-road camping is not permitted. There are hundreds of campsites and RV parks along the Gulf Coast. Reservations are recommended during the winter high season. For more information, contact the Florida Campground Association, 1638 N Plaza Drive, Tallahassee, FL 32308-5323. ✆ 850/562-7151 .

CANOEING

Canoe rentals are available in many locations, and offer an exciting way to see the real Florida. You can paddle down backwaters that are inaccessible to any other means of transport, and commune with nature and the spectacular wildlife. There are hundreds of miles of paddling to be had around the islands and along designated trails in the state parks. Use an effective insect repellent and good sunscreen when canoeing. Before setting out, you should also check on the conditions likely to be encountered and decide whether you have the necessary skills to cope with them. Always be alert to tides, weather and wind changes.

CLOTHING AND PACKING

The rule is: pack light and wear light. Florida is one of the few destinations where you can get away with a single piece of carry-on luggage if you are flying. Unless you are staying in a very smart resort or like to dress up for dinner, T-shirts and shorts suit most people during the day, with slacks or jeans and a casual shirt or blouse being ideal for the balmy evenings. Sandals are fine for wearing around the pool and on the beach, and are sometimes essential as the sand can literally get too hot to walk on with bare feet. If you plan to spend time walking, pack a comfortable pair of shoes or trainers.
Although the temperature drops a few degrees after sundown, most visitors still find it warm, even on winter evenings. That said, a light jumper is advisable, if only to cope with icy blasts from the air-conditioning. You will need swimwear, sunglasses and a hat. The sun is deceptively strong, especially if there is a cooling sea breeze, and sunglasses not only help you to see better in the glare, but will also protect your eyes from harmful rays. Finally, you only have to spend a short time in Florida to appreciate how useful a baseball cap is.

CURRENCY *

*For Overseas visitors

The American dollar comes in denominations of $1, $2 (rare), $5, $10, $20, $50 and $100. In practice, it is not a good idea to carry the higher denomination bills and some establishments will not accept them. Always keep a few $1 bills handy for tips. It is easy to confuse the various denominations as they are all the same size and colour, the only immediate difference being their face value, although notes of different value do carry different portraits. Always check that you are handing over the right note,

Fact File

and check your change, although it must be said that most people would never dream of short-changing you.

The dollar is divided into cents, with the following coins: 1¢ (a penny), 5¢ (a nickel), 10¢ (a dime) and 25¢ (a quarter). There are 50¢ and $1 coins but these are not often found in circulation – although they do make good souvenirs!

Most major credit cards are widely accepted, particularly American Express, Diners Club, Visa and Mastercard. There may occasionally be problems in submitting foreign Access cards, but these are usually overcome if you point out that Access is part of the Mastercard network. There is little point in taking all your credit cards with you, so pick one or two that will be most useful or will allow you the greatest credit, and leave the rest at home.

If taking traveller's cheques, make sure they are dollar cheques as these can be handed over in lieu of cash in most places.

American Express can be contacted round the clock on ✆ 1-800-528-4800.

CUSTOMS AND IMMIGRATION*

Customs

*For Overseas visitors

There are strict customs and Department of Agriculture regulations governing what can and cannot be imported into the United States. Drugs, dangerous substances, firearms and ammunition are banned, as are a wide range of foods (such as meat, dairy products, fruit and vegetables) in order to maintain the disease-free status of Florida's agriculture. Florida does have rabies, however, so pets being brought into the state either from abroad or elsewhere in the USA should be vaccinated against the disease before arrival.

While there are no restrictions on how much cash you can take into the USA, all amounts over $10,000 must be listed on your customs declaration form. This is part of the authorities' fight against drug-trafficking. All gifts taken into the country, and their value, should also be listed on the customs declaration form, and should not be wrapped so that they are available for inspection if required. Duty is not payable if the total value of gifts and goods is under $400.

You are allowed to import duty-free into the USA: 200 cigarettes or 50 cigars or 2kg of tobacco, or proportionate amounts of each; and 1 litre of alcoholic drinks (if aged twenty-one or over). If arriving by air from outside the USA, you will have to hand in your customs declaration form after clearing immigration and picking up your checked-in luggage. You can buy duty-free goods at the airport before departure, but you cannot pick up your purchases until just before you board the plane. After paying for your goods, you will be given a receipt, and you must then remember to collect your goods from the duty-free staff, who will wait for you between the exit gate and plane.

Immigration

All visitors to the USA must have a valid passport with at least six months to run from the day they are scheduled to return home. Under the Visa Waiver Program, visitors from the UK, most EU countries and Japan arriving by air or sea aboard a carrier participating in the programme do not require a visa, provided they do not plan to stay for more than ninety days. If travelling under this programme, you must complete a green 'visa-waiver form', which is handed to you at check-in and which you hand in to the immigration officer together with your passport. Visitors with a valid visa must complete the white visa form.

Visitors making frequent trips to the USA or planning to stay for more than three months should have a valid visa. Visa application forms can be obtained from embassies and some travel companies, and must be posted together with your passport, photographs and any other documents to the visa section of the United States Embassy in your country. Allow at least twenty-one days for processing, although the visa is often returned earlier than this. Some travel companies offer fast-track visa services in conjunction with the embassy. The normal tourist visa allows multiple entries to the US and is now valid for ten years. Indefinite visas granted some time ago are now being cancelled by US Immigration officers as you enter the USA, so that you have to re-apply for the new ten-year visa, or switch to 'visa-waiver' entry.

Immigration procedures have been improved at most entry airports, but delays can be lengthy if, for instance, two 747s arrive within a few minutes of each other. On arrival in the immigration hall you will be allocated to a queue and must stay behind the line marked on the floor until called by the immigration officer. You may be asked to show your return air ticket to prove you plan to leave. Your passport will then be stamped with a date by which you must leave the country. A portion of the immigration form is stapled to your passport, and this has to be surrendered when leaving the country, so do not lose it.

Note: Immigration officers now insist that white visa and green visa-waiver forms are filled in correctly, and have the power to impose fines (rarely used) if they are not. Make sure your forms are filled in correctly, and if you make a mistake get another from the cabin crew.

CYCLING

Cycling is a great way to explore the state, and cyclists are well catered for. It has two advantages: the countryside is flat, and you are more likely to get into the laid-back Florida lifestyle by gently pedalling around than by motoring. There are many bicycle-rental shops, and bicycle stands are often provided so that you can leave your locked bike while you go to the beach, shop or eat.

DISABLED VISITORS

Florida leads the world in the provision of facilities for the disabled. By law, all public buildings and national and state parks must provide access facilities for the disabled, and most hotels, resorts and attractions mirror this with superb access and facilities. There are also special provisions for the totally or partially blind or deaf. Many of the major car-rental companies can provide specially adapted cars and vans if given advance notice. The *Florida Services Directory for Physically Challenged Travellers* is a useful booklet which lists relevant associations and facilities throughout the state. It is available from the Florida Department of Commerce Warehouse, 126 Van Buren Street, Tallahassee, FL 32399-2000. ✆ 904/487-1465.

DRIVING*

*For Overseas visitors

A valid driving licence is needed if you want to hire a car in Florida, and you must be twenty-one years of age or over. If you plan to spend a lot of time in the state it may well pay you to get a Florida driving licence, which is valid throughout the USA. You can usually walk into a driving test centre and join the queue to take the written and practical exam, providing you have proof of identity, such as birth certificate.

Many overseas automobile clubs are affiliated with the American Automobile Association (AAA), and proof of membership of one of these entitles you to a range of services, including breakdown assistance, free maps and discounts for car hire, hotels and many attractions.

Driving in Florida is a pleasure once you become used to driving on the right-hand side of the road and have familiarized

Above: You are never far from a golf course in Florida and visitors are welcome
Below: Ball games are very popular on some beaches

Fact File

yourself with traffic signs and so on. Because of the lower speed limits, wider roads and generally good lane discipline, foreign drivers should have no problems. It also helps if you can remember that even-numbered roads generally run from east to west, while odd-numbered highways usually run from north to south. Use an Interstate highway if you want to get somewhere in a hurry.

Car Hire

It is usually cheaper to arrange your car hire through your travel company or as part of a fly-drive package. Although it is optional, you are strongly advised to have collision damage waiver (CDW), and it is often cheaper to pre-pay this as well.

If flying in to Tampa or Miami, the hire companies are situated on the airport or a short drive away. If travelling from outside the airport, courtesy buses shuttle to and from the car pick-up point. At the car-hire check-in, hand over your driving licence, proof that you are twenty-one or over (such as your passport) and your pre-paid voucher if you have one. You will be asked for an address where you will be staying; if you are touring, give the hotel or motel where you will be staying on the first night. If paying by voucher, you will also be asked for a credit card to pay for incidentals such as airport tax, additional drivers and so on.

Don't be persuaded to upgrade or take out unnecessary insurance. Be sure you understand what they are trying to sell you, and then decide if you need it. Cars range from economy models to limousines, and some rental companies will urge you to upgrade because they have run out of vehicles in the category you ordered. If you upgrade, they will charge you for a bigger car, but if you refuse they will be obliged to give you a bigger car at their expense.

Car-hire Companies

Alamo
✆ 1-800-327-9633.
Avis
✆ 1-800-331-1212.
Budget
✆ 1-800-527-0700.

Dollar
✆ 1-800-421-6868.
Hertz
✆ 1-800-654-3131.
National
✆ 1-800-227-7368.
Thrifty
✆ 1-800-367-2277.

Accidents

If you are involved in a road accident, exchange particulars with other drivers and get the names and addresses of any witnesses.

You must report to the police any accident that involves personal injury or significant damage (anything other than a minor bump). Never admit liability or say 'I'm sorry', which may be taken as an admission of responsibility. Some insurance companies will not honour a policy if a driver has admitted liability. If you are driving a rented car, notify the hire company as soon as possible. If people are injured, leave medical assistance to those who are qualified to administer it; if you try to help and something goes wrong, you could face a massive bill for damages.

Drink-driving

Even having an open container of alcohol in a car is illegal, and it is just not worth the risk of drinking and driving. If convicted, the penalties are very severe, including imprisonment and vehicle confiscation. Driving under the influence of drugs is also a serious crime and you will probably end up in prison if you are caught.

Breakdown

If you break down in a rural area, move onto the hard shoulder, lift the bonnet (hood), and then get back into the vehicle, lock the doors and wait for help. If you break down at night, you must use your emergency flashers. Police cars cruise the highways and will come to your aid. If there is an emergency phone on the road, use that to call for assistance. If you are a member of an overseas motoring organization that is affiliated to the AAA, you can ring toll-free (1-800-AAA-HELP. If you are driving a rental car, notify the hire company as soon as possible so that a replacement can be provided.

Gas (Petrol)

All cars now run on unleaded fuel, but filling up can be confusing as pumps operate in a number of different ways. Read the instructions on the pump. Usually the nozzle has to be removed and the bracket on which it rests then moved into an upright position to activate the pump. Some filling stations require pre-payment, some accept credit cards which can be inserted into the pump (a receipt is provided), some will only accept cash and others charge more for fuel paid for by credit card.

Parking

When parking at night, choose a spot that is well lit and, ideally, in a busy area. Lock all doors and make sure anything of value is out of sight.

Rules of the Road

- Always drive on the right and pass on the left.
- Buckle up – seat belts are compulsory.
- Observe the speed limits: generally 55–65mph (88–104kph) on highways; 5–40mph (40–64kph) in urban areas; and 15mph (24kph) in school zones. There are on-the-spot fines for speeding, and if you are caught going too fast you could spend a night in jail. If you are stopped for speeding, don't pay the police officer, but instead pay fines direct to the relevant Clerk of the Court. Handing money to a police officer might be misinterpreted as a bribe.
- Report all traffic accidents.
- If a school bus stops with its flashers on, traffic in both directions must stop while children get on or off. Traffic can only move when the bus moves off. The only exception is when oncoming traffic is separated from the bus by a central reservation, in which case it can proceed.
- Do not park near a fire hydrant. You will be fined and may be towed away.
- Always give way to emergency vehicles.
- U-turns are legal in Florida, unless there is a sign to the contrary.
- When it starts to rain, turn on your headlights and windscreen wipers and reduce your speed.
- Don't pick up hitchhikers.

ELECTRICITY*

***For
Overseas
visitors**

Electrical appliances operate on a 110-volt, 60-cycle alternating current. Plug adaptors will be needed if you are bringing dual or universal voltage appliances from Europe, as electrical appliances designed for 220–240V will be damaged if used on this power supply.

EMBASSIES AND CONSULATES*

US Embassies Abroad
Australia
36th floor, Electricity House,
Park and Elizabeth streets,
Sydney NSW 2000.
© 02-261-9200

Canada
1155 Saint Alexandra,
Montreal, Quebec H22 122.
© 514-398-9695

New Zealand
4th floor, Yorkshire General
Building, CNR Shortland and
O'Connell, Aukland.
℗ 09-303-2724

UK: 5 Upper Grosvenor Street,
London W1A 2JB.
℗ (0171) 499 7010

Foreign Embassies and Consulates in Florida

There are no embassies and most consular offices are in Miami,
usually operated by a local businessman from his office. Contact
telephone numbers:

Belgium ℗ 305-932-4263
Denmark ℗ 305-446-0020
France ℗ 305-372-9799
Germany ℗ 305-358-0290
Italy ℗ 305-374-6322

Japan ℗ 305-530-9090
Holland ℗ 305-789-6646
Norway ℗ 305-358-4386
Spain ℗ 305-446-5511
UK ℗ 305-374-1522

(no consul for Australia or
New Zealand)

There are also consular offices in Orlando for:

UK
200 South Orange Avenue,
℗ 407-426-7855

Holland
400 South Orange Avenue,
℗ 407-425-8000

France
522 East Washington Street,
℗407-294-5844

***For
Overseas
visitors**

EMERGENCY TELEPHONE NUMBERS*

For the police, fire and ambulance emergency services, dial 911.
If that fails, dial 0 for the operator.

HEALTH *

Visitors are not likely to face any serious health problems, although they should take precautions against the sun and biting
insects (such as sand flies and mosquitoes), both of which can
ruin a holiday. If bitten by any animal, wild or domestic, seek
medical attention as rabies is endemic in Florida. There are also
some poisonous snakes and spiders, but their bites are rarely
dangerous if treated promptly, and such bites are, in any case,
uncommon. Other minor problem areas include one or two
nasty species of wasp. Be careful around coral and be alert for

jellyfish and spiny sea urchins, which are occasionally a problem at certain times of the year.

Immunization is not required unless you are travelling from an infected area.

Most hotels and resorts have doctors on call around the clock, and emergency dental treatment is available at all times. There are also a number of walk-in clinics which provide emergency treatment, and if the situation is really serious you can drive straight to the nearest hospital's emergency room. Procedures for payment vary, but if you have insurance ring the company's information line and seek advice. It may be that you have to pay for treatment on the spot, in which case you must make sure that you retain all receipts for when you put in your claim.

Pharmacies will make up valid prescriptions from mainland US doctors, but it is recommended that visitors from Europe bring in prescribed medicines together with a covering letter from their doctor.

Drinking water from the tap is perfectly safe, although bottled mineral and distilled water is widely available.

Safe Tanning

The sun is very strong but sea breezes often disguise just how hot it is. If you are not used to the sun, take it carefully for the first two or three days, use a good sunscreen of Factor 15 or higher, apply it frequently, and do not sunbathe during the hottest parts of the day when the sun is highest in the sky. Wear sunglasses and a sun hat. Sunglasses will protect you against the glare, especially strong on the beach, and a sun hat will protect your head. Remember that continued exposure to strong sun can cause eye cataracts and that eyelids are especially vulnerable to skin cancer. Remember also that it is even more important for children to take things carefully at first by covering up.

If you spend a lot of time swimming or scuba-diving, take extra care as you will burn even quicker with the combination of salt water and sun. Calamine lotion and preparations containing aloe are both useful in combating sunburn.

Insect Bites

Mosquitoes can be a problem almost anywhere. If you find them in your room, burn mosquito coils or use one of the many electrical plug-in devices that burn an insect-repelling tablet. Mosquitoes are not so much of a problem on or near beaches because of the onshore winds, but they may well bite you as you enjoy an evening meal in the open air. Use a good insect repellent, especially if you are planning trips inland through forested areas.

Sand flies can be a problem on the beach. Despite their tiny size (they are known locally as 'no-see-ums') they can give you a nasty bite. Fire ants are common, and their bites can be very irritating. As ants of all sorts abound, make sure you check the ground carefully before sitting down!

INSURANCE*

It is absolutely essential to have adequate insurance cover. It is a good idea to carry a photocopy of your insurance policy with you at all times, keeping the original in your room. While medical service is first rate, it can be expensive, and awards in the court for damages as a result of an accident can be astronomic.

MEDIA*

US national and international newspapers are readily available, although the latter are usually quite expensive. Cable and satellite television normally provide between forty and sixty stations.

NIGHTLIFE

There is a wide range of evening entertainment on offer, from theatres and concerts to zany nightclubs and piano bars. You can dine out and enjoy live entertainment at many of the large hotels and resorts, or mingle with the locals in waterside bars and clubs. Many bars and restaurants have live music which is supplied by small groups or solo musicians. You can enjoy comedy or listen to jazz, country and western or hard rock, or dance the night away until the early hours.

PHOTOGRAPHY

The intensity of the sun can play havoc with your films, especially if you are photographing near water or white sand. Compensate for the brightness or your photographs will come out overexposed. The heat can actually damage film, so store reels in a box or bag in the hotel fridge if there is one. Remember to protect your camera when you are on the beach as a single grain of sand is all it takes to jam it; if you leave it unprotected it may also be stolen. When buying film, always make sure that its

Fact File

*For Overseas visitors

expiry date is still a long way off. Many outlets offer a one-hour film-processing service, and it is a good idea to have early films developed so that you can check that your exposure meter readings are correct.

POLICE*

In an emergency, dial 911.

POST*

Many shops, hotels and resorts sell stamps, but it is often advisable to avoid stamp machines as these can work out more expensive. Post offices can handle all your mailing requirements, and even sell you special packaging if you want to ship gifts and purchases back home.

A first-class airmail letter to anywhere in the US costs 32¢ and a postcard 20¢. A postcard sent airmail to the UK or mainland Europe needs a 40¢ stamp, while an airmail letter costs 50¢.

US Mail boxes are painted blue and bear the US Mail logo. Although not immediately obvious, they can be found in most shopping areas. To post a letter, pull down the handle and deposit your mail in the tray. There are usually also posting facilities in hotels.

PUBLIC HOLIDAYS, ANNUAL EVENTS AND FESTIVALS*

January
January 1 (New Year's Day): public holiday.
Martin Luther King Day: third Monday

February
President's Day: third Monday

May
Memorial Day: last Monday

July
Fourth of July: Independence Day celebrations at various locations

September
Labor Day: first Monday

October
Columbus Day: second Monday

November
Armistice-Veteran's Day: 11th
Thanksgiving Day: last Thursday

December
Christmas Day: 25 December

SECURITY

There is no evidence to show that holiday-makers face any greater risk in Florida than they do in many other places world-wide, and the Gulf Coast in particular has comparatively low levels of serious crime. It makes sense, however, to take a few basic precautions:

● Do not wave money about, wear as little jewellery as possible, and keep money, credit cards and passport separate from one another.

● Before leaving the airport, make sure you know where you are going and which route you are taking. The car-hire company will supply you with a map and directions, and signposting from airports has been much improved in the last few years. If it is very late and you are tired, consider taking a taxi to an airport hotel and stay overnight so that you can continue your journey the next day when you are feeling refreshed and it is daylight.

● If you are staying in a hotel or motel, use their safe or the in-room safe (if provided) for valuables such as jewellery, extra money, tickets and passports. Carry a photocopy of your passport's ID page in case you are asked for identification.

● When travelling in a car, keep the doors locked and the windows up, and when leaving the car parked, make sure that nothing is visible that might tempt a thief. Never sleep in the car overnight; always find a cheap hotel or motel. When parking your car at night, try to leave it in an area where there is good lighting.

● Ask the hotel staff or your holiday courier if there are any areas to avoid, and make sure you do not stray into them, especially late at night. It really is quite safe to walk around, but there is always the outside chance that your bag or video camera may be snatched.

● If you are stopped or threatened, do not resist. Most thieves only want cash or easily disposable items, and most will make their getaway as soon as you hand these over. If you are robbed, report the incident to the police immediately. Report the theft of credit cards and traveller's cheques to the appropriate organizations, and if your passport is stolen, report the loss as soon as possible to your embassy or consulate. The photocopy of the ID page will speed up the replacement.

Theft and Lost Property

If luggage or property is lost or stolen, report the incident to the police and relevant authority (airport, car-hire company, hotel and so on) as soon as possible. Get a theft report from the police and contact your insurance company for permission to replace any stolen items, keeping all receipts if you do so.

SHOPPING

Most shops are open from 9am to 5pm Monday to Saturday, while stores in shopping malls often stay open until 10pm and later and In tourist areas, some stores never close. There is a huge range of goods to choose from T-shirts and trainers to local arts and crafts and antiques. Prices are usually much lower than in Europe and there are great bargains to be had.

Remember that sales tax (about 7% although it varies from county to county) is added on by the cashier and is not shown on the price label.

SPORTS

Boating

There are hundreds of boats of all shapes and sizes available for charter, either bareboard or fully crowded. Thousands of visitors choose to bring their own boats and there are many public boat ramps.

Diving

Florida is a great place to learn how to scuba-dive and snorkel as it has warm, clear waters and many top dive schools. Snorkelling skills can usually be acquired after about fifteen minutes' tuition, and all you need is a mask and snorkel for breathing, and flippers for propulsion. Scuba-diving requires training to learn technique and how to use the complicated equipment. Instruction by qualified teachers can lead to a certification which entitles you to dive anywhere in the world. A four-day course is usually adequate to certify for open-water diving.

Fishing

Fishing is almost a way of life in Florida, where people fish for both food and sport. Florida saltwater and freshwater fishing

Fish Catches in Florida

Amberjack:	**15–75lb (7–34kg)** January to May.
Barracuda:	**7–35lb (3–16kg)** year round.
Bonefish:	**5–15lb (2–7kg)** April to October.
Cobia:	**20–90lb (9–40.5kg)** November to April.
Dolphin:	**5–60lb (2–27kg)** March to November.
Grouper:	**5–80lb (2–36kg)** year round.
King mackerel:	**8–70lb (3.6–31.5kg)** September to May.
Blue marlin:	**120–400lb (54–180kg)** April to December.
White marlin:	**45–85lb (20–38kg)** May to December.
Permit:	**8–40lb (3.6–18kg)** April to June.
Sailfish:	**15–70lb (7–31.5kg)** October to May.
Sharks:	**20–1,000lb (9–450kg)** year round.
Snapper:	**1–20lb (0.45–9kg)** year round.
Snook:	**6–35lb (3–16kg)** year round.
Tarpon:	**25–200lb (11–90kg)** March to July.
Tuna:	**8–200lb (3.6–90kg)** October to August.
Wahoo:	**15–70lb (7–32kg)** October to July.
Redfish:	**3–20lb (1.3–9kg)** July to December.

Fact File

licences are needed for all out-of-state anglers aged sixteen or over. Florida residents do not need a licence if they are saltwater fishing from the land or a pier. All fees collected are used specifically for improving and restoring fish habitats, building artificial reefs, researching marine life and habitats, and for enforcement and education. Licences are obtained from county tax-collector offices and local fishing and bait shops.

Fishing charters and cruises are widely available throughout the area. It is often best to go in a group or be prepared to join one as this cuts down the cost. Most charters include the cost of the boat, equipment, bait and guides. For information on fishing, species and catch sizes allowed, contact the Department of Natural Resources, Office of Fisheries Management & Assistance Services, Mail Station # 240, 3900 Commonwealth Boulevard, Tallahassee FL 32399-3000.
© 905/922-4340.

Some fishing don'ts:
● Don't damage or take coral.
● Don't disturb marine mammals.
● Don't take turtle eggs.
● Don't take or harvest queen conch.
● Don't exceed catch limits.
● Don't use spearguns within 90m (300ft) of public beaches and piers or in prohibited areas.

Golf

There are hundreds of courses, many of them at championship standard, and scores are open to visiting players.

Tennis

There are plenty of opportunities for a game either at public courts or at those run by the larger hotels and resorts. If you want to play tennis, book courts early in the morning or late in the afternoon for the first few days until you aclimatize to the sun, and remember to drink lots of fluids both during and after the game.

Watersports

There is probably a greater choice of watersports in Florida than anywhere else, and there are hundreds of shops selling and renting equipment. Many hotels and motels offer free use of equipment or will rent it out, and there are opportunities to learn a wide range of activities from qualified instructors throughout the islands.

Yachting

The calm, warm waters attract vessels from around the world, and there are many full-service marinas. Most of these offer docks and yacht slips if you want to spend a few days ashore, and there are thousands of craft available on short- and long-term charters either with or without crew.

SUNBATHING

Almost all Florida counties have laws which ban topless sunbathing or nudity on public beaches. A few counties established nudist beaches in remote areas but even these have proved controversial and as a result of complaints, many have reverted to costume compulsory areas. The police enforce the law quite strictly.

TAXES*

Sales tax causes a lot of confusion among foreign visitors, who find they are asked to pay more for goods than the amount printed on the price tag. Sales tax varies from county to county but averages about seven per cent, while local authorities can levy their own additional county tax of up to one per cent. These levies are added automatically when you pay. Most goods are subject to this sales tax, but groceries and medicines are exempt, as are services 'that do not involve the sale of a tangible item', such as legal and accounting services. Hotel taxes are additional to the sales tax.

*For Overseas visitors

TAXIS*

Taxis are plentiful and reasonably priced, and are a sensible option if you want to wine and dine outside your hotel. They also offer a safe way of travelling around late at night.

TELEPHONES*

The emergency number for police, fire and ambulance services is 911. Area codes are only used when dialling between areas. Direct dialling of calls, even international ones, is possible from hotels, motels and most public phone boxes. Local calls cost 25¢. For international calls, dial the international code (011), followed by the country code, then the area code less the leading zero, and finally the local number. Most public phone boxes have instructions on how to place and dial international calls. If paying by cash, you will need a stack of quarters; it is easier to use your credit card or to reverse the charge (a collect call). Dial 411 for local directory enquiries, or the area code 555-1212 for long-distance numbers.

TIME AND DATES*

North-western Florida operates under Central Time, while the rest of the state is one hour ahead on Eastern Time – the same time as in New York and five hours behind Greenwich Mean Time. Daylight Savings Time comes into effect on the first Sunday of April, when the clocks go forward one hour; they go back one hour to Standard Time on the last Sunday in October.

Americans abbreviate dates by writing the month first, followed by the day and year. So, Christmas Day 1999 is written 12.25.99.

***For
Overseas
visitors**

TIPPING*

In restaurants, tip fifteen per cent (or higher if you have had exceptional service) unless a service charge is automatically added to your bill. If there is an automatic service charge and you do not think the service was good, complain and refuse to pay this charge. Wages in the catering trade are low and staff rely on tips to boost their take-home pay. It is customary to tip porters $1 for every piece of large luggage carried, and hotel maids $1 for each night they clean your room.

TOILETS (REST ROOMS)*

These are better known in the US as rest rooms, bathrooms, men's rooms or ladies' rooms. Public toilets are found almost everywhere. There are frequent rest areas with toilets along the main highways, and you will also find toilets in shopping malls, fuel stations, restaurants, attractions and so on. Many stores even offer their own toilet facilities for shoppers.

TOURIST OFFICES

Overseas and Out-of-state Offices

Canada
US Travel and Tourism Administration, Suite 602, 480 University Avenue, Toronto, Ontario M5G 1V2
✆ 416-595-5082

UK
United States Travel and Tourism Administration, PO Box 1EN, London W1A 1EN
✆ (0171) 495 4466

USA
US Travel and Tourism Administration, US Department of Commerce, Washington DC 20230
✆ 202/659-6000

Tourism Enquiries

Attractions
Florida Attractions Association
✆ 904/222-2885

Hotels and motels
Florida Hotel/Motel Association
✆ 904/224-2888

National and state parks
US Forest Service, Tallahassee
✆ 904/681-7265 (forests);
904/488-9872 (parks)

Local Tourist Offices
Bradenton Area Convention and Visitors Bureau (CVB)
PO Box 1000,
Bradenton FL 34206
✆ 813/729-9177

Citrus County Tourist Development Council
1300 South Lecanto Highway, Lecanto FL 34461
✆ 904/746-4223

Clearwater/Pinellas Suncoast Welcome Center
3550 Gulf to Bay Boulevard, Clearwater FL 34619
✆ 813/461-0011

Clearwater Beach Welcome Center
41 Causeway Boulevard, Clearwater Beach, FL 34630.
✆ 813/461-0011.

Emerald Coast CVB
PO Box 6098 Fort Walton Beach, FL 32549
✆ 904/651-7131

Lee County CVB
PO Box 2445, Fort Myers, FL 33902
✆ 941/338-3500

Marco Island and Everglades Convention and Visitors Bureau
1102 North Collier Blvd, Marco Island, Fl 33937
✆ 941/394-7549

Naples Area Tourism Bureau
PO Box 10129, Naples, Fl 33941
✆ 941/262-2712

**Navarre Beach Area
Chamber of Commerce**
PO Box 5336,
Navarre Beach, FL 32566
© 904/939-3267

Panama City Beach CVB
PO Box 9473,
Panama City Beach FL 32417.
© 904/233-6503.

**Pasco County Office
of Tourism**
7530 Little Road, Room 202
New Port Richey, FL 34654
© 813/847-8990

Pensacola CVB
1401 E Gregory Street,
Pensacola, FL 32501
© 904/434-1234

It covers the Gulf Breeze Area
Chamber of Commerce
© 904/939-2691, Perdido Key

Chamber of Commerce
© 904/4924660 and Santa Rosa

Island Authority
© 904/939-2691

**Pinellas Suncoast
Welcome Center**
2001 Ulmerton Road,
Clearwater FL 34662
© 813/573-1449

**St Petersburg-Clearwater
Area Convention and
Visitors Bureau**
Florida Sunset Dome,
1 Stadium Drive, Suite A,
St Petersburg

FL 33705-1706.
© 813/464-7200

Sarasota CVB
655 North Tamiami Drive,
Sarasota FL 34236
© 941/957-1877

**South Santa Rosa
County Tourist
Development Council**
PO Box 5337,
Navarre, FL 32566
© 904/939-2691

**South Walton Tourist
Development Council**
PO Box 1248,
Santa Rosa Beach, FL 32459
© 904/267-1216

**Suwanee County Tourist
Development Council**
PO Drawer C,
Live Oak, Fl 32060
© 904/362-3071

Tallahassee Area CVB
200 West College Avenue,
Tallahassee, FL 32302
© 904/413-9200

**Tampa and
Hillsborough CVB**
111 Madison Street, Suite
1010, Tampa FL 33602
© 813/223-2752

WEIGHTS AND MEASURES*

Americans still use the imperial system of weights and measures, although metric measurements are becoming more common. Road distances are always given in miles, while petrol (gas) can be in either gallons or litres, or both. Liquid measures differ between America and Britain: 1 US gallon = 0.833 imperial gallons = 3.8 litres.

*For Overseas visitors

Women's clothes sizes in the US are two sizes less than the UK equivalent, while women's shoe sizes in the US are labelled two sizes larger (in other words, a size 6 in the UK would be a size 8 in the US). Men's shoe sizes in the US are one size larger than in the UK (in other words, a size 10 in the UK is a size 11 in the US).

LANDMARK VISITORS GUIDES

Practical guides for the independent visitor

Written in the form of touring itineraries

Full colour illustrations and maps

Detailed Landmark FactFile of practical information

Landmark Visitors Guides highlight all the interesting places you will want to see, so ensuring that you make the most of your visit

AVAILABLE SHORTLY:

1.Britain

Cotswolds &
  Shakespeare Country

Devon

Dorset

Edinburgh

Guernsey

Hampshire/Isle of Wight

Jersey

Lake District

Peak District

Scotland

Yorkshire Dales & York

2.Europe

Bruges

Black Forest

Alps and Jura

Provence

Italian Lakes

Gran Canaria

Norway

Madeira

Tenerife

3.Other

India: Kerala and The South

New Zealand

Orlando & C. Florida

Florida: The Keys

Florida: Atlantic Coast

LANDMARK
Publishing Ltd ● ●●●

Waterloo House, 12 Compton, Ashbourne,
Derbyshire DE6 1DA England

NOTES

INDEX

Published by:
Landmark Publishing Ltd,
Waterloo House, 12 Compton, Ashbourne
Derbyshire DE6 1DA England

1st Edition

ISBN 1 901522 01 6

British Library Cataloguing in Publication Data:
a catalogue record for this book is available
from the British Library.

Colour Origination: AD VER srl, Italy
Print: Tipolitografia Petruzzi, Corrado +C, Italy
Cartography: Mark Titterton
Design: Mark Titterton

Picture Credits:
Author
Bradenton Area CVB   Busch Entertainment Corp.
Destin/Ft Walton TB   Florida Tourism
Great Miami C&VB   Homasassa Springs State Wildlife Park
International Photo Bank pp 22,54,63(both),74,103,122
Lee Island Coast V&CB   Naples Area TB
Panama City Beach TB   Pinellas Sun Coast TB
Sarasota CVB   St Lucie County TDC
St Petersburg/Clearwater Area CVB   Tallahassee TB
Tampa/Hillsborough C&VA

Cover Picture
Front; St Pete's Beach, International Photo Bank
Back; Panama City Beach TB